# ISLE OF MAN TRANSPORT

## A COLOUR JOURNEY IN TIME

STEAM RAILWAYS, SHIPS AND ROAD SERVICES BUSES

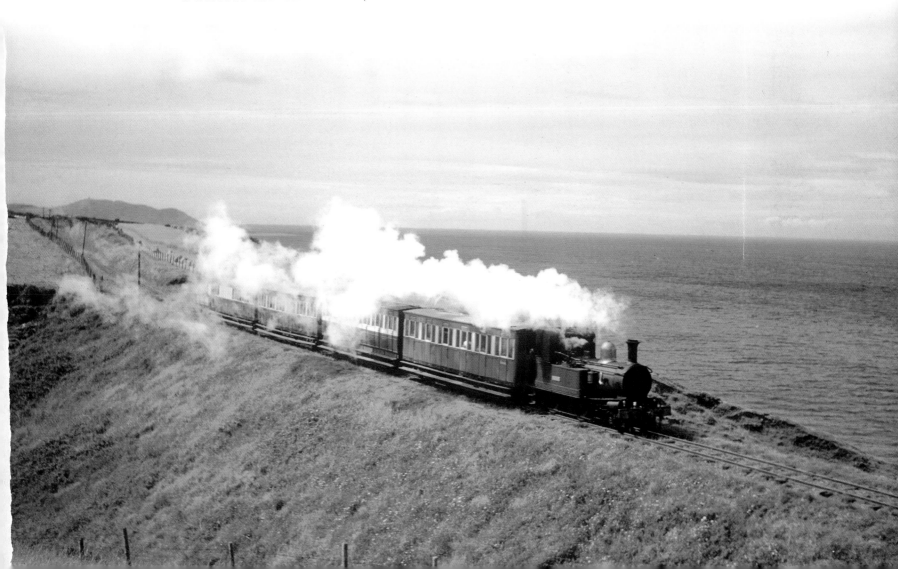

# ISLE OF MAN TRANSPORT

## A COLOUR JOURNEY IN TIME

STEAM RAILWAYS, SHIPS AND ROAD SERVICES BUSES

MARTIN JENKINS & CHARLES ROBERTS

PEN & SWORD
TRANSPORT

First published in Great Britain in 2017 by
Pen & Sword Transport
An imprint of Pen & Sword Books Ltd
47 Church Street
Barnsley
South Yorkshire
S70 2AS

ISBN 9781473862470

Typeset in Palatino by Pen & Sword Books Ltd
Printed and bound in China by Imago

Pen & Sword Books Ltd incorporates the imprints of Pen & Sword
Archaeology, Atlas, Aviation, Battleground, Discovery, Family
History, History, Maritime, Military, Naval, Politics, Railways, Select,
Social History, Transport, True Crime, and Claymore Press, Frontline
Books, Leo Cooper, Praetorian Press, Remember When, Seaforth
Publishing and Wharncliffe.

For a complete list of Pen and Sword titles please contact:
Pen and Sword Books Limited
47 Church Street, Barnsley, South Yorkshire S70 2AS, England
E-mail: enquiries@pen-and-sword.co.uk
Website: www.pen-and-sword.co.uk

**Cover photo:**
In Castletown, the Isle of Man Railway runs alongside the main Douglas–Port
Erin road and provides a good vantage point for photographs. With impressive
smoke effects, No. 13 *Kissack* heads towards Port St Mary with a five-coach
train on 27 June 1976. (Andrew King)

**Title page:**
On 19 August 1960, No.10 *G.H.Wood* heads a northbound four-coach train
for Ramsey near Gob-y-Deigan on the east coast of the Island. As much of this
section of the former Manx Northern Railway ran through sparsely-populated
areas, a number of halts and stations were closed over the years, including a
short-lived one located somewhere near here. (Les Folkard/Online Transport Archive)

**Back cover:**
On 1 August 1953, No. 3 *Pender* is at Douglas ready to couple up to a train for
Ramsey. (John McCann/Online Transport Archive)

Groudle Glen Railway 2-4-0T locomotive *Polar Bear* at The Headland at the end
of the 1958 season. (Phil Tatt/Online Transport Archive)

This classic shot of Isle of Man Road Services Leyland PD2 No. 63 was taken
outside Laxey Garage on 17 May 1964. When withdrawn in 1970 it was sold to
a dealer in the UK. Laxey Garage was closed in 1969.
(R. L. Wilson/Online Transport Archive)

Dressed overall, Isle of Man Steam Packet Company *Ben-my-Chree* (IV) of 1927
is ready to depart from Victoria Pier for Dublin on 3 August 1953. To the left of
her prow are the steps leading down to the cross-harbour ferry.
(John McCann/Online Transport Archive)

# INTRODUCTION

**This book is dedicated to the memory of the late John McCann who, like both authors, hailed from Merseyside and who, like us, had a life-long fascination with most forms of transport on the Isle of Man. During his life, John made numerous visits taking many hundreds of photographs. Now his collection of negatives, colour slides and ciné films resides with Online Transport Archive. Whilst answering a request from an author to locate some slides for a book it became clear to us that John's Isle of Man coverage deserved a wider audience, especially his initial batch of 100 or so quality Kodachrome I images taken in 1953. He had photographed the island's ships, railways and tramways, and some of his views of the Douglas Corporation horse trams, Manx Electric Railway and Snaefell Mountain Railway will appear in a later volume.**

The photographs in this book cover the period 1953–79. These were the years during which visitor numbers to the Island declined dramatically. As a result, the Isle of Man Steam Packet fleet was reduced, several routes were discontinued and traditional steamers were replaced by roll on-roll off ferries. The Isle of Man Railway stopped carrying freight, ended schools traffic, terminated its sparse winter timetable, closed the lines to Peel and Ramsey, reduced its stable of locomotives and, for a period, operated no trains in or out of Douglas. Isle of Man Road Services acquired second-hand buses, reduced services and introduced one-man operation. On the credit side, more people used Ronaldsway Airport; the railway line from Douglas to Port Erin survived and was marketed as a major tourist attraction after it was taken over by the Government, as were the bus routes operated by Isle of Man Road Services.

As many books have been published detailing the history of the Island's various forms of transport, our volume does not go into major historical or technical detail, although some background information is included in some of the captions. Suffice to say that, for many years, the Island relied upon the Isle of Man Steam Packet Company and the Ramsey Steamship Company for passenger and freight connections with the rest of the British Isles, and many of these companies' vessels appear in the book.

The first part of the rail network opened between Douglas and Peel in 1873, and many views of all lines, including those abandoned in 1968, are featured, as well as each of the locomotives still in use in 1953. The first motor bus-service was introduced in 1907, with major development occurring in the late 1920s, and most of the motor-bus types operated by Isle of Man

**This book** is dedicated to John McCann. In this portrait, he was taking in the Manx sun at Port Soderick on 4 September 1967, during one of his many visits to the Island. *Mair McCann/Online Transport Archive*

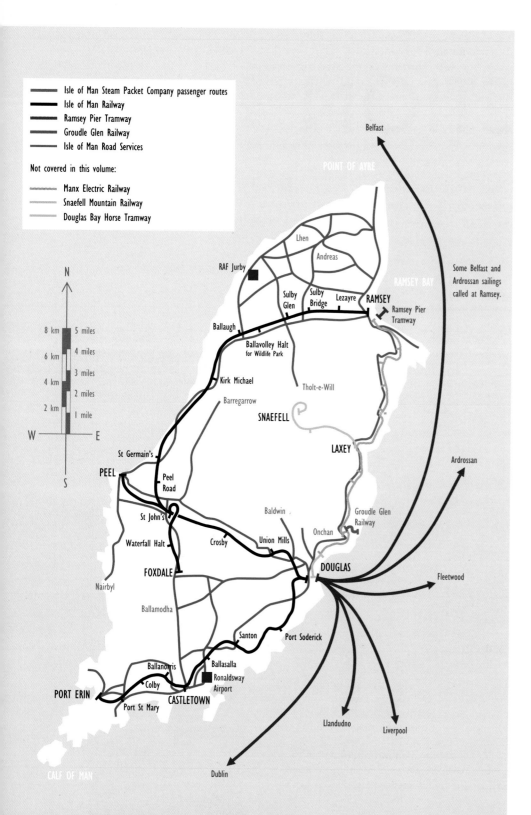

Isle of Man Steam Packet Company passenger routes
Isle of Man Railway
Ramsey Pier Tramway
Groudle Glen Railway
Isle of Man Road Services

Not covered in this volume:

Manx Electric Railway
Snaefell Mountain Railway
Douglas Bay Horse Tramway

Road Services, a subsidiary of the Isle of Man Railway, are well illustrated. We are also pleased to include rare views of the Groudle Glen Railway taken in the 1950s, as well as a few scenes on the Queen's Pier Tramway at Ramsey.

We do not know when John McCann first visited the Island, but each of us remembers the first time we encountered all the delights on offer to the transport enthusiast.

**Martin:** 'My first visit was one summer towards the end of the 1940s – I can't remember the exact year, but I think it was probably 1948. The crossing from Liverpool was, to say the least, lively. The boat was pitching and tossing about in a very heavy swell, and, all around my mother and me, people were being ill and throwing up over the side. "Just keep looking straight ahead" my mother instructed.

'Feeling somewhat weak and exhausted, we finally reached Douglas and somehow managed to stagger down the gangplank onto the quay with our suitcases. By now the sun was shining. I remember we boarded a horse tram and rode almost the full length of the Prom, but I can't recall the name or the whereabouts of our hotel. However, I do remember having kippers for breakfast as well as the strict routine surrounding meal and bath times, and the long walk to the toilet.

'During our stay, we only used public transport so almost every day we would ride the horse tram back towards the town centre. On one occasion, I am sure we went upstairs on one of the double-deckers. If only I had started taking notes. On two occasions we made "the round trip" as my mother called it – out to Ramsey on the Manx Electric and then back to Douglas by train. On one of these "marathons" I think we spent time at Glen Wyllin and explored Kirk Michael. I was fascinated by the stations with no platforms, the movements through the passing loops, the antiquated carriages with their "steps" and why some trains had two engines.

'On one day, my mother let me spend time at Douglas Station just watching. It was on this occasion that I saw several cattle wagons arrive with the animals bellowing and stamping. I had seen similar sights in and around the Birkenhead Docks. However, my biggest thrill was being taken on the footplate of one of the Manx Peacocks as it shunted round the yard. "Don't tell your mother – or anyone else" I was warned. During our stay we made several quite long bus journeys (usually on wet or dull days), but I can't recall where we went, although I do remember walking round St John's and then catching a bus. We also toured the island – I think in a Bedford OB. I have always had a soft spot for these vehicles. We also made the obligatory trip up Snaefell, and I can still picture the timeless comings and goings at Laxey, and persuading my mother to ride back in an open trailer despite it being wet and cold. My mother was not amused. At some point, I also remember the conductor collecting the mail and the bags being loaded into a waiting GPO van at Douglas.

'Again, I was left to watch the goings on at Derby Castle for most of one afternoon. It was great to be able to stroke the horses as they waited to be walked round. I was also intrigued by the trailer movements on the MER (Manx Electric Railway). Fortunately, the crossing back to Liverpool was calm as a millpond and I already knew I wanted to go back, but this would not happen until 1956.'

**Charles:** 'Like Martin, my earliest memories of the Isle of Man began with Steam Packet sailings from Liverpool, but in my case they were about twenty years later. The first trip was in 1968 and we returned several times after that until the early 1970s, staying with family friends in Onchan – Gladys and Cyril. People don't have names like that today! Nearby was the new Onchan Stadium and a treat was a round of pitch and putt golf. On one occasion, having trounced me over the first 16 holes, my dad gave me strict instructions on stance and posture at the 17th tee, resulting in a hole-in-one and a round of applause from the rather impatient queue of golfers behind us. My sporting prowess peaked at the age of eight.

'Our ships to and from the island were usually the side-loaders from the 1960s, *Ben-my-Chree* or *Manx Maid*, but I remember vividly a spring bank holiday weekend relief sailing from Liverpool on *Snaefell*. This is one of the worst crossings I have ever experienced anywhere and, although I'd acted on advice and found myself a below-deck seat in the centre of the vessel, that was

to no avail when I went up on deck for fresh air and immediately threw up.

'I'm pretty sure that on the 1968 trip we did the island circuit by steam railway from Douglas to Ramsey, and back by Manx Electric, but the family had no camera with us on that trip. My first photographic efforts began with a Box Brownie in 1972, but the film was a total failure because of my lack of understanding of the shutter settings.

'Our hosts' bungalow in Onchan provided a good vantage point to watch the regular Douglas Corporation route which terminated across The Park. My memory of Road Services trips to remoter parts of the island include the archaic ticket machines, which I subsequently discovered were "Insert Setrights" bought cheaply second-hand by the General Manager from UK operators who were modernising.

'The unpleasant trip on *Snaefell* put me off sailing. To my regret, I left it over 20 years before paying a return visit. Some things had changed but an awful lot was very familiar and nostalgic, the trams, trains, hotels and weather particularly. I have much the same feeling every time I visit.'

## Companion volume

The authors hope the nostalgic colour images featured in this book will have revived many pleasant memories. Work on a companion volume is well underway. Due to be published in 2018, this will feature an equally evocative selection of colour views but this time covering aviation, the Manx Electric Railway and Snaefell, Douglas Corporation's iconic horse trams and its idiosyncratic bus fleet, and a few other subjects which we haven't managed to squeeze into this volume. Together we hope the two volumes will provide comprehensive coverage of the Island's unique mix of transport over the years.

## Acknowledgements

The authors wish to thank all those who have provided photographs for this book. Particular thanks are due to: Leo Sullivan of Boston, USA, who helped to make the Donald Nevin collection available; David Postle of the Kidderminster Railway Museum for providing access to the Jim Jarvis collection of railway slides; Chris Poole for preparing the map and Peter Waller for undertaking much preliminary scanning.

Significant help in checking caption detail has been given by Bill Barlow, Nigel Bowker, Jonathan Cadwallader, Brian Faragher and Rob McCaffery. As with the authors' other transport-related books, this volume has been compiled in conjunction with Online Transport Archive (OTA), a UK-registered charity dedicated to the preservation and conservation of transport images, and to which the authors' fees have been donated.

For further detailed information about the archive, please contact the Secretary at 25 Monkmoor Road, Shrewsbury SY2 5AG (email: secretary@onlinetransportarchive.org).

**Today, residents** and visitors travel to and from the Island by sea and by air. Before the first steam-powered vessel called at the Island in 1815, all travel had been on sailing packets, principally from Liverpool or Whitehaven. To offer residents an improved service, a Manx Company was formed in 1830 that, two years later, became the Isle of Man Steam Packet Company (IOMSPCo) whose function was to maintain regular links with the UK for residents, tourists, cargo, coal and mail. This view from Douglas Head taken in July 1971 shows the main harbour facilities at Douglas with the King Edward VIII Pier (foreground) and the Victoria Pier to the north. At the piers are representatives of the IOMSPCo fleet with their distinctive black and red 'Cunard-style' funnels. (Brian Patton)

**Over the** years, the Company has operated many passenger vessels, of which the oldest to be captured in colour appears to be the triple-screw steamship *Victoria* (1641GRT [Gross Register Tonnage]). Launched in 1907 by William Denny & Bros for the South Eastern & Chatham Railway, *Victoria* was sold to the IOMSPCo in 1928, after which she worked mostly on secondary services or advertised excursions. After serving as a troop carrier during the Second World War, the ship was reconditioned and remained in service until the end of the 1956 season, after which she was scrapped at Barrow. In this view she was at Douglas on 3 August 1953. Many years earlier, her overall appearance had been improved with removal of the cowls from the tops of her funnels. (Jim Jarvis/Online Transport Archive)

**Certain names** have been reused over the years; for example, the first *Ben-my-Chree* dated from 1845. The fourth *Ben-my-Chree* is seen at Douglas in August 1953. Built by Cammell Laird of Birkenhead in 1927, this handsome twin-screw steamship (2586GRT) was the first new vessel to be acquired by the IOMSPCo after the First World War. Powered by Parsons single-reduction steam turbines, the oil-burning steamer was capable of a speed of 23 knots. Built with a largely enclosed upper deck and improved saloon and steerage accommodation including sleeping quarters, 'The Ben' had a crew of 82 and could carry 2586 passengers. Following distinguished war service that included troop carrying and participation in the evacuation from Dunkirk (1940) as well as the D-Day landings (1944), she was refitted and rejoined the Company fleet. During this time, her single funnel was shortened and the cowl removed. (John McCann/Online Transport Archive)

**Captain Griffin** stands on the bridge of 'The Ben' on the occasion of her last ever crossing, which was from Douglas to Liverpool on 13 September 1965. After this, the ship was briefly renamed *Ben-my-Chree II* so that the Company's new carry ferry could take her name. After nearly 40 years' service, 'The Ben' left Liverpool for breakers in Belgium in December 1965. (G. W. Price)

**The next** vessel to arrive was named *Lady of Mann* after the title held by the Duchess of Atholl, who performed the launch ceremony at Vickers-Armstrongs in Barrow-in-Furness in March 1930. Fitted with similar equipment to the *Ben-my-Chree*, this large twin-screw steamer (3104GRT) could also achieve a speed of 23 knots. During the Second World War she often worked in tandem with '*The Ben*' as a troop ship, taking part at Dunkirk and also during the D-Day landings. After the war she was reconditioned by Cammell Laird and like '*The Ben*' was mostly used at times of peak demand, when her capacity to carry 2873 passengers with 81 crew proved invaluable on busier crossings. Shown here in July 1959, she is waiting to sail to Douglas from the giant floating landing stage at Liverpool. After making her last sailing on 17 August 1971, '*The Lady*' returned to her birthplace at Barrow before sailing to a breaker's yard on the Clyde. She was 41 years old. (Donald Nevin)

**As already** indicated, IOMSPCo vessels played a vital role during the Second World War, with eight of the fleet being involved in the mass evacuation of British and Allied troops from Dunkirk. Four vessels were lost: *King Orry* (built 1913), *Mona's Queen* (built 1934) and the twins *Fenella* and *Tynwald* (built 1937). To begin replenishing their fleet, the Company placed an order with Cammell Laird for the first of six sister ships that became known as the 'King Orry' class. Entering service between 1946 and 1955, these were essentially modified versions of the 1937 vessels. The twin-screw steamer *King Orry* (2485GRT), the fourth ship to carry the name, set the pattern, with her raked stern, single cowl-topped funnel, two masts and improved accommodation which included private cabins which could be reserved in advance. She had a crew of 68, could carry 2136 passengers and was capable of 21 knots, power being provided by the Company's preferred single-reduction geared turbines. Here, '*The Orry*' is leaving Fleetwood in 1971, just a few days after a seasonal service to Douglas had been reintroduced after a gap of some ten years. This fine ship made her final voyage four years later on 31 August 1975 and was eventually broken up at Strood in 1979. (Peter Deegan)

**The** *Mona's Queen* (IV) which entered service in 1946 was virtually identical to '*The Orry*' although she was licensed to carry slightly more passengers. She was photographed here at Douglas in May 1953. Her career with the IOMSPCo proved short-lived. After sailing mostly to Fleetwood or Liverpool, her duties were partially displaced in 1955 when the more economical *Manxman* and the recently refitted *King Orry* assumed responsibility for the two boat Douglas–Liverpool winter service. On 11 September 1961, '*The Queen*' had nearly 1200 passengers on board when she undertook the last sailing from Fleetwood for ten years, the service being suspended owing to the unsafe state of the wooden landing berth. Five days later she made her last-ever voyage for the Company, after which she was offered for sale. Although newer than the two surviving pre-war vessels, she carried fewer (2163, plus 68 crew) and the Company also believed she would fetch a better price. After being laid up at Barrow for much of 1962, she was renamed *Barrow Queen* and left for Piraeus at the end of that year. Subsequently, she had various names before being broken up as the *Fiesta* in 1981. (Jim Jarvis/Online Transport Archive)

**Delivered in** 1947, *Tynwald* (V) (2490GRT) was virtually identical to her earlier sisters except for the provision of additional windows on the promenade deck. She was licensed to carry 2393 passengers and could achieve a speed just in excess of 21 knots. *Tynwald* made her final sailing on 26 August 1974 having suffered serious damage to her turbines. She was broken up the following year in Spain. In this view she is alongside Victoria Pier in August 1953. (Jim Jarvis/Online Transport Archive)

**The fourth** of the six sisters, *Snaefell* (V), entered service in 1948 and was again almost identical to the other members of the class. She made her final voyage on 29 August 1977, after which she was laid up in Birkenhead Docks until sold for scrap in 1978. Here she backs out of Douglas Harbour in May 1953. For generations of travellers, these classic ships were often referred to as 'little liners' or 'little Cunarders' on account of their red and black funnels. Note the Manx coat of arms on the bow and the location of the triple-chime steam whistle on the upper front of the funnel. (Jim Jarvis/Online Transport Archive)

*Mona's Isle* (V) (2491 GRT), the fifth member of the *'King Orry'* class, entered service in 1950 and was the last IOMSPCo steamer to be fitted with low-pressure turbines. Operated by a crew of 67, she had accommodation for 2268 and although very similar to *Snaefell*, she had no Manx crest on her bows. Here she is steaming between Douglas and Liverpool on 9 July 1955. She was the first Company vessel to sail to the new Fleetwood facilities in August 1971. As visitor numbers to the Island declined, it became impractical for the IOMSPCo to retain vessels for limited seasonal use. Although she starred in the highly successful film *Chariots of Fire* in 1980, and also undertook the Company's 150th anniversary cruise round the island, *Mona's Isle* was withdrawn after sailing from Douglas to Llandudno on 27 August 1980. She was broken up shortly afterwards. Her passing also marked the end of any excursion sailings by the Steam Packet Co. from Liverpool to Llandudno. (John McCann/Online Transport Archive)

**The sixth** and final sister did not arrive until 1955. Although outwardly similar to the others, *Manxman* (II) had a different engine room configuration in order to accommodate her Pametrada turbines. She is seen here in 1961 at Douglas, about to depart for Llandudno. Her funnel cowl was then still in place, but, as with others of this class, this was subsequently removed. (Phil Tatt/Online Transport Archive)

**During 1981** and 1982, *Manxman* attracted considerable attention as she was by then the last traditional Isle of Man boat and the last classic steamer operating within British waters. This fine broadside view was taken as she prepared to enter the Birkenhead dock system for her winter lay-up. *Manxman* made her final historic voyage from Douglas to Liverpool on 4 September 1982. Sold initially for static use at Preston Docks, she sailed there from Liverpool with passengers aboard for one last time on 3 October 1982. The Preston venture proved unsuccessful, as did subsequent periods back in Liverpool and at Hull. A concerted preservation attempt failed and she was eventually broken up in Sunderland in 2012. A much-loved class of vessel had finally passed into history. (Nigel Bowker)

**To meet** changing patterns of travel, four car-carrying vessels entered service during the years covered by this book. These were designed so that motorists could drive on and off safely, and efficiently at all states of the tide and from all ports then served by the IOMSPCo. Spiral ramps linked to the car deck as well as doors located either side of the hull enabled vehicles to drive on and off at the relevant level. These 'side-loaders' effectively revolutionised travel to and from the Island. The first to arrive was *Manx Maid* (II) (2724GRT). Launched by Cammell Laird in 1962, she had a service speed of 18 knots and was powered by steam-turbine engines. *'The Maid'* was the first IOMSPCo vessel to be fitted with anti-roll stabilisers although these did little to alleviate the unpleasant sensation of pitching in rough seas. This view shows her berthed at Liverpool on 8 April 1968. *'The Maid'* made her last sailing on 9 September 1984 after which she was withdrawn and finally broken up in 1985.

(E. J. McWatt/Online Transport Archive)

*'The Maid'* was licensed to carry 1400 with a crew of 60, and up to 90 cars and light commercial vans, but no heavy lorries or containers. This view shows the top of the spiral ramps filled to capacity with predominantly British-built vehicles, including the photographer's Bedford CA camper van. In the past, a limited number of cars and other vehicles, including new buses, had been carried on the Company steamers, but it could take an hour to winch them on and off at either end. Furthermore, the number of licensed passengers also had to be reduced according to the number, weight and disposition of the assembled vehicles. (Phil Tatt/Online Transport Archive)

**The second** of the car carriers, the *Ben-my-Chree* (V) (2762GRT) made her maiden voyage on 12 May 1966. This was the fourteenth and last IOMSPCo vessel to be built in Birkenhead by Cammell Laird and the last to have separate classes of accommodation. She differed from '*The Maid*' in a few minor details, perhaps the most noticeable being her flat, as opposed to raked, top to the funnel. In this view, she is in Douglas in June 1977. Faced by competition from a rival ferry company that was offering an efficient roll on-roll off service, the IOMSPCo decided to withdraw both '*The Maid*' and '*The Ben*', with the latter making her final scheduled crossing on 19 September 1984. However, owing to a shortage of vessels to handle the 1985 TT traffic, she was chartered back from her new owners for the period 25 May to 9 June. During these few precious days, many enthusiasts managed to make a last sentimental voyage on a classic steam-powered passenger vessel. Then destined for a new career in the USA, this deal fell through and, after four years of neglect in Birkenhead Docks, she was broken up in Spain in 1989.
(Brian Faragher/Online Transport Archive)

**The third** of the car ferries, *Mona's Queen* (V) (2998GRT) was built by Ailsa Shipbuilding of Troon. This view was taken in August 1972 shortly after she had entered service. In a move to reduce running costs, she was the first IOMSPCo vessel to be powered by more economical diesel engines. She was also fitted with the latest equipment to improve manoeuvrability. She had a crew of 55, and could take up to 100 cars and vans. Although there was just one class of passenger accommodation, there was still a preponderance of wooden-slatted seats. It was this vessel which inaugurated new car ferry services to Dublin (1974) and Fleetwood (1976). After being withdrawn as surplus to requirements in 1990, '*The Queen*' spent several years in Birkenhead Docks before being renamed *Mary the Queen* in 1995, after which she sailed under her own power to the Philippines for conversion into a night ferry. She ended her days with Indian breakers in 2005. (Nigel Bowker)

**The final** new vessel to be delivered during the period covered by this book was *Lady of Mann* (II) (2990GRT). Launched in 1976, she was virtually identical to *Mona's Queen,* although she was fitted with more powerful engines that gave her a top speed of 23 knots and a reputation as a 'speed merchant'. On both the Ailsa-built 'side-loaders' the funnel was a dummy, housing emergency generators. Shown here on 21 June 1977, 'The Lady' is at anchor in the Mersey, dressed overall to mark the Queen's Silver Jubilee. The black paint on the exhaust vent, which also doubled as the mainmast, was lower than on her sister ship. In 1989 she underwent a major refit when her car-carrying capacity was increased. Latterly, she was often used as a standby vessel, whilst at other times chartered out for cruise work. Eventually, she was sold to Greek owners in 2005 who converted her into a stern loader, which increased her length considerably. As the *Panagia Soumela* she ended her days in 2011 at a Turkish breakers. (Allan Clayton/Online Transport Archive)

**For freight,** the Isle of Man relies heavily on its sea transport links to and from the UK and Ireland. Traditionally, most goods have been handled at Douglas, and to a lesser extent Ramsey, but there are several smaller ports dotted around the Island. At 502ft above sea level, Corrins Hill provided a perfect vantage point for this panorama of Peel Harbour taken on 22 May 1959. (Marcus Eavis/Online Transport Archive)

**Castletown and** Port St Mary are two of the island's other minor ports. In the first view, the inner harbour at Castletown was viewed from Castle Rushen on 24 May 1959. In the second, fish were being off-loaded at Port St Mary on 31 August 1968. Fishing is a long-standing industry and Manx kippers enjoy a much-deserved reputation. (Marcus Eavis/Online Transport Archive; John McCann/Online Transport Archive)

**At Douglas,** heavier goods were normally handled on the main harbour piers whilst smaller cargoes were dealt with in the upper harbour by various freighters including those operated by the IOMSPCo. In this memorable view taken in May 1953, the upper harbour quays are seen at low tide flanked by shipping offices, warehouses, hotels and other facilities. The vessel on the left is *Glen Strathallan,* registered in Douglas. She was laid down as a steam trawler by Cochrane & Sons of Selby, but the company who placed the order went into liquidation. She was then purchased by Mr R. Colby Cubbin and converted into a private yacht at a cost of £30,000. After wartime service and further use as a training ship, she was eventually scuttled in Plymouth Sound for use as a dive site. The motor coaster in the centre of the photo is the *Indorita,* belonging to Coppack Bros & Co. of Connah's Quay in North Wales. She was built in 1920 by Abdela & Mitchell at Queensferry on the Dee for steel makers John Summers & Co. She survived until 1974, before being towed to Spain for scrap. Other vessels visible include the Isle of Man Harbour Commissioners' wooden steam barge *Sirdar* of 1898, the dive boat *Perragh,* the passenger motor launch *Karina* of 1913 and the IOMSPCo's steam coaster *Conister.* Also shown are many of the scores of small rowing boats which were available for hire during the season.

(Jim Jarvis/Online Transport Archive)

**The first** new, as opposed to second-hand, freighter acquired by the IOMSPCo was *Peveril* (II) (798GRT). Built by Cammell Laird in 1929, she had triple-expansion machinery, a single funnel, two masts and could carry any cargo from coal to cattle. Here she is seen in Coburg Dock, Liverpool, in the 1950s. The vessel was withdrawn in 1964 and broken up at Glasson Dock. The Company normally assigned the name *Peveril* to its principal freighter, with four different vessels carrying the name over the years. (G. H. Hesketh)

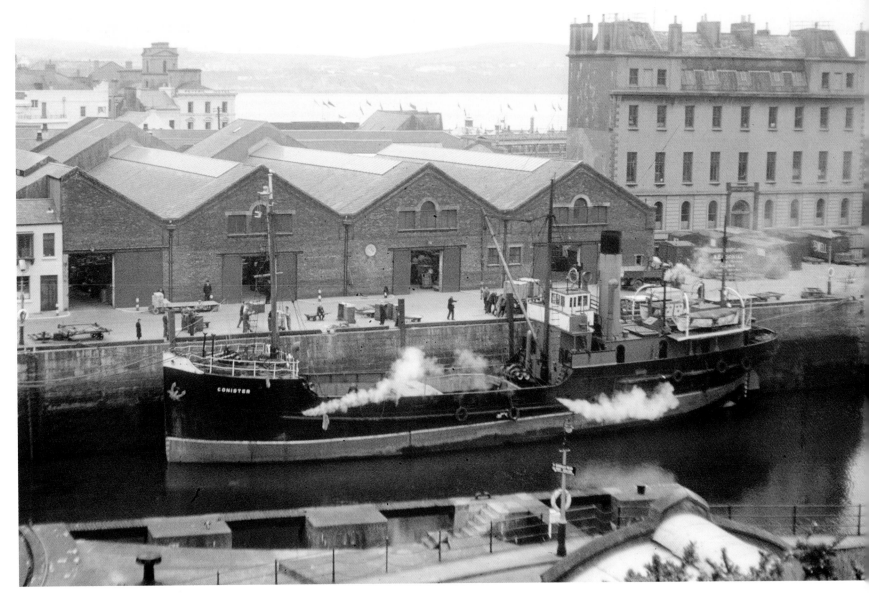

**The Company** had a history of buying second-hand cargo ships. These included *Abington* (411GRT), which had been built and engined in Hull in 1921. After being purchased by the IOMSPCo in 1932, she was renamed *Conister* after the Conister Rock, the home of the Tower of Refuge in Douglas Harbour. She had triple-expansion engines aft, and two masts and derricks forward of her funnel. In this view she is seen in the upper harbour at Douglas in 1962. For over 40 years this small cargo carrier made numerous crossings of the Irish Sea until finally going for scrap in early 1965. (Allan Clayton/Online Transport Archive)

**It was** not until 1951 that the IOMSPCo invested in a diesel-powered cargo ship. Built by the Ailsa Shipbuilding Company, *Fenella* (III) had engines supplied by British Polar Engines Ltd. She could carry up to 750 tons, with her large flush deck aft accommodating cars, vans and lorries. However, the rapid rise in containerisation saw her sold to Greek owners in 1973. Four years later she caught fire and sank. Here she is shown in Coburg Dock, Liverpool, in November 1971, just months before the dock closed and when the Company freight operations were transferred to Hornby Dock. (Nigel Bowker)

*Peveril* (II) and *Conister* were replaced by two more Ailsa-built motor vessels. Entering service in 1964, *Peveril* (III) (1048GRT) had the same engines and equipment as *Fenella* (III), and approximately the same carrying capacity, but she differed by having her machinery and accommodation located aft. With a speed of some 12 knots and a crew of 14, she was a regular on the Douglas–Liverpool service, carrying cattle, containers, general merchandise and vehicles. She was photographed at Douglas in July 1970 when her two on-deck cranes were busy handling the blue containers owned by the Company, most of which had been acquired second-hand from British Railways. Following withdrawal in 1981, she was owned by various Mediterranean shipping lines and renamed no less than eight times before being scrapped in 2001. (Brian Patton)

**The other** replacement vessel entered service in 1965. Smaller than *Peveril* (III), *Ramsey* (II) had less powerful engines and was designed so she could serve most of the Island's ports. On 28 August 1966 she is seen here at her home port of Ramsey tied up alongside the Steam Packet offices on the East Quay. Being unsuitable for conversion into a container ship, she only lasted a relatively short time and was sold in 1973. After a spell on the south coast of England, she made the long voyage to the Cape Verde Islands. At some point she was converted into a tanker and was still active as late as 2015, but is now probably withdrawn. (Brian Faragher/Online Transport Archive)

**To handle** the rapid growth in container traffic, facilities on the North Quay at Douglas were upgraded to include a 28-ton derrick and improved warehouse accommodation. An additional container ship, *Spaniel,* was chartered then purchased from The Belfast Steamship Company in 1973, being renamed *Conister* (II). Built as the *Brentfield* (891GRT) by George Brown of Greenock in 1955, she was powered by Sulzer engines. She is shown on 2 July 1978, approaching Douglas with a stack of Steam Packet containers visible on deck. During the 1970s, *Peveril* (III) and *Conister* (II) could carry up to 125,000 tons annually. However, at the end of the period covered by this book, the IOMSPCo was facing strong competition from swifter, more efficient roll on-roll off freighters operated by a new rival company. The two vessels were withdrawn in 1981, with *Conister* (II) going for demolition later that year. They were replaced indirectly in 1983 by a large, second-hand end-loading roll on-roll off freighter (1975GRT) which was named *Peveril* (IV). (Andrew King)

**Another familiar** vessel in Manx waters was *Mannin* (127GRT), a small, coal-fired dredger. Owned by the Isle of Man Harbour Board, she was painted light grey with a yellow and black funnel, and was built by Lobnitz of Renfrew in 1936. She was powered by a reciprocating two-cylinder compound steam engine. Her job was to remove silt and sediment from the channels giving access to the Island's various ports. This view of her was taken in Douglas in July 1959 and shows her on-deck crane which was used to lower and raise the grab hopper. Sold in 1972 to a company in Port St Mary, and then to the Lancaster Port Commission in 1974, she sank in the Manchester Ship Canal in 2006. (Donald Nevin)

**The Island's** second major port is Ramsey, located at the mouth of the Sulby River. The first view, taken on 27 August 1966, shows the local shipbuilding yard which, for many years, had its own cradle which ran on rails, and was used to raise and lower ships in and out of the water. The second view, taken on 26 May 1959, focuses on the site of the former Ramsey Quay Tramway, which from the early 1880s provided a direct link from the West Quay onto the rail network at Ramsey Station. This made it a main supply route for exports and imports, especially coal, which was taken from the quayside for distribution to the various locomotive sheds. After carrying heavy traffic during the Second World War, the increased use of lorries led to the tramway being out of use by 1952 and the track lifted by 1957. No trace remains today. The fishing boat was registered in Whitehaven and the swing bridge on the right provides access to the North Quay. (Allan Clayton/Online Transport Archive: Marcus Eavis/Online Transport Archive)

For a century until it ceased to trade in 2014, the Ramsey Steamship Company (RSSCo) operated a fleet of coastal steamers. Known affectionately as 'The Ben' boats on account of the prefixes to their names – Ben meaning girl or lady in Manx – these sturdy ships served all the Island ports, handling cargoes such as imported coal, sand, cement, oil, liquid-petroleum gas, grain, agricultural produce, and the export of ore, lead, gravel, stone and salt. There now follows some representative views of the RSSCo fleet, including the *Ben Maye*, which was the oldest to be captured in colour. Launched in 1921 in Leith by J. Cran & Somerville Ltd as the *Tod Head* (323GRT), she was powered by two-cylinder compound engines and acquired by the RSSCo in 1955, who named her *Ben Maye* (Yellow Lady). This view was taken at Ramsey in August 1964, just months before she was sold for scrap. (G. W. Price)

**One steamer** which had a long career with the RSSCo was the *Ben Ain* (Our Lady) (266GRT). She had similar engines to the *Ben Maye*, but was launched by the Manchester Dry Docks Co. of Ellesmere Port for Thomas Brothers Shipping Company of Liverpool in 1924 and named *Doris Thomas*. After another change of name and owner, she was acquired by the RSSCo in 1938 and finally sold for scrap in 1963. She had a top speed of 8 knots and is here seen at Douglas in July 1959. Note her open wheelhouse. All the RSSCo vessels had black funnels sporting a white Maltese cross on a red band and either black or grey hulls. The house flag was blue with a Maltese cross in the middle and the letters R S S C in the corners. (Donald Nevin)

**Representing the** new generation of motor vessels first introduced in 1956 with acquisition of the *Ben Rein* (III) is the *Ben Vooar* (III) (Big Lady) (472GRT), which arrived in 1959. Launched in Holland in 1950 as *Mudo*, she had six-cylinder oil-fired engines and was capable of a speed of 9 knots. She was disposed of after running aground in 1975, but was later repaired and following several changes of owner was eventually declared a 'constructive total loss' in 1984. Here, she is seen loading at Douglas on 23 August 1966. This *'Ben'* had superior accommodation for the captain, who was also able to control her engines from the bridge following the installation of new equipment. This enabled the Company to cut costs by reducing the number of crew.
(Brian Faragher/Online Transport Archive)

**The** *Ben Varrey* (III) (Mermaid or Girl of the Sea) (451GRT) was ordered new from a Dutch yard. Launched in 1963, she was fitted with eight-cylinder oil engines and is seen here on 17 July 1972 at Douglas South Quay, having unloaded her cargo. After developing major engine problems, she was withdrawn in 1984 and scrapped the following year. (Hamish Stevenson)

**The** *Ben Veg* (Little Woman or Wife) (346GRT), which was smaller than the other motor vessels, was designed to cope with the restrictions at Castletown and Laxey harbours. Launched by Clelands Shipbuilding Co. of Wallsend and fitted with six-cylinder oil engines supplied by Blackstone & Co., she commenced trading in 1965. After completing nearly 1000 voyages, a gradual loss of traffic, including the bulk delivery of grain to Laxey Harbour, resulted in her being laid up in 1978. This little ship ended her days in the West Indies and is believed to have sunk whilst under tow in 1991. She is shown in Castletown Harbour on 11 September 1968. (Brian Faragher/Online Transport Archive)

**Acquired in** 1971 and named *Ben Veen* (II) (Darling Girl), this vessel (486GRT) was launched as *Plover* from Richards (Shipbuilders) of Lowestoft for the General Steam Navigation Company in 1965. Powered by six-cylinder oil engines supplied by W. H. Allen, Sons & Company of Bedford, she was disposed of in 1984. After striking a submerged object, she sank in heavy seas whilst carrying grain from Rouen to Great Yarmouth in 1988. Here she is leaving Douglas on 5 July 1981. (Andrew King)

**The final** vessel operated by the RSSCo during the years covered by this book was the *Ben Ain* (II) (500GRT), which is shown at Ramsey on 4 July 1980. Launched in Holland as *Deben* for the Blue Star Line in 1966 and fitted with six-cylinder oil engines supplied by Blackstone & Co. of Stamford, she was acquired by the RSSCo as the *Gretchen Weston* in 1976, and remained in the Company fleet until sold in 1991 for further service in Cyprus and the Eastern Mediterranean. She was scrapped under the Bolivian flag as *Abdoulah I* in 2001. (Andrew King)

**The fleet** of vintage locomotives still running on the Isle of Man allows people of all ages to soak up the sights, sounds and sensations of the steam age. The surviving operational locomotives come from a one-time fleet of fifteen 2-4-0 tank engines delivered by Beyer, Peacock & Co. of Manchester between 1873 and 1926. Over the years, some have been withdrawn, some put into long-term storage, some restored, and some rebuilt and reboilered. Before we cover the Island's rail network in detail, these next views provide portraits of each of the locomotives captured in colour. No. 1 *Sutherland* was one of the three engines delivered in 1873 for the opening of the 11½ mile line from Douglas to Peel. It was named after the Duke of Sutherland, who was Chairman of the Isle of Man Railway Company. During its life, this locomotive was associated mostly with the Peel and Ramsey lines, and was often shedded at Ramsey. In 1891, it was fitted with a new boiler, and then in 1919 and 1923 received boilers from other locomotives, and finally in 1934 with the boiler from No. 7 *Tynwald*. Delivered in 1923, this was one of two special 'Bradshaw' boilers which were named after the-then locomotive superintendent, James Bradshaw. These had Ross 'Pop' safety valves, one of which was located in the top of the dome and the other on top of the first ring of the boiler, as seen in this view taken in August 1953. *Sutherland* was withdrawn in September 1964, probably due to the poor state of the boiler, by then some forty years old. After a spell in store, it was one of a group of disused locomotives to be placed on static display at St John's in 1967. Following a further period of inactivity, No. 1 was housed in the new railway museum at Port Erin in 1975. In 1998, the locomotive returned to service carrying the refurbished boiler from No. 8 *Fenella* and, for a period, operated special trains on the Manx Electric Railway. Since 2003, No. 1 has again been in store, but is expected to move back to Port Erin Museum once some cosmetic restoration has taken place.

(John McCann/Online Transport Archive)

**No colour** picture of sister locomotive No. 2 *Derby*, which was withdrawn in 1951, has come to light.

**The third** of the initial batch of locomotives was to have been *Viking*, but, in fact, carried the name *Pender*, after Sir John Pender, a financial entrepreneur who eventually became Chairman of the Company. This early trio set the pattern for future orders, although with minor variations. They weighed approximately 20 tons and had sloping smokeboxes, Salter safety valves, inclined outside cylinders, highly-polished 'bell-mouth' domes, copper-capped chimneys complete with brass fleet numbers on either side, one-piece curved cabs, small 2ft 10¾in diameter boilers pressured to 120psi and small 320-gallon side tanks. Each was capable of hauling up to fifteen fully-laden four-wheel carriages on gradients as steep as 1:65. During its life, *Pender* received two new boilers and then, in 1951, was fitted with the refurbished 'Bradshaw' boiler previously carried by No. 2 *Derby* since 1923. As on No. 1, this had a Ross 'Pop' safety valve concealed in the top of the dome and another on the first ring of the boiler. This view taken in August 1953 also shows the rectangular spectacle plates at the front and the smaller, round ones at the rear. The footplate crews always complained that the cab area on these first locomotives was too cramped. After being withdrawn in August 1959, *Pender* was stored until eventually returned to the UK twenty years later to be exhibited at the Manchester Museum of Science and Industry, where it has been sectionalised to show visitors its internal workings. (John McCann/Online Transport Archive)

**To work** the new 15½ mile line from Douglas to Port Erin, Nos 4–6 arrived from Beyer, Peacock during 1874/5. Although equipped initially with the same diameter boilers as Nos 1–3, they had 385-gallon water tanks, needed for the distances and gradients on the new line. They had 'bell-mouth' domes, Salter safety valves and rectangular spectacle plates both front and back in the cab. Named *Loch* after the Lieutenant Governor, Henry Brougham Loch, No. 4 was rebuilt in 1909 in order to give it the same tractive effort as later locomotives Nos 10–13. This involved fitting a larger 3ft 3in diameter boiler and higher side tanks, increasing capacity to 480 gallons. In this view taken in August 1953, it is fitted with the refurbished 1914 boiler from No. 5 *Mona* which it had carried since 1946. Subsequently out of service for many years, the locomotive received a brand-new boiler built by Hunslet of Leeds in 1968 at which point the original safety valves were replaced by the Ross 'Pop' variety and the dome was closed off. No. 4 was one of the engines in regular service during the late 1960s and early 1970s, and remained in service until 1995. After public fundraising, *Loch* returned to service in 1998, but has been in store since 2015 with an expired boiler certificate. (John McCann/Online Transport Archive)

**Delivered from** Beyer, Peacock in 1874, No. 5 was named *Mona*, after the Latin word for the Isle of Man. New boilers were fitted in 1895 and 1907, and then, in 1914, it was upgraded in order to achieve the same tractive effort as Nos 10–13. This was done by fitting a larger-diameter boiler and enlarged side tanks similar to those on *Loch*. In 1926, it was given the refurbished 1911 boiler from No. 6 *Peveril* and then in 1946 a brand-new boiler was supplied by Beyer, Peacock, at which point the Salter safety valves were replaced and a smaller, cast-iron chimney was fitted. Small fleet numerals were also positioned above the nameplates on each side as seen in this view taken in August 1953, although these were later removed. Long associated with the Northern lines, *Mona* was withdrawn at the end of the 1968 season and later sold to the UK-run Isle of Man Railway Society, although kept on Isle of Man Railway (IMR) premises. Today, it remains in store at Douglas. (John McCann/Online Transport Archive)

**As shown** here, the nameplates on Nos 4 and 5 were split LO CH and MO NA so as not to have the lettering obscured by the original injector overflow pipe. The pipes were later moved, but the nameplates retained their unusual spacing. The nameplates are also placed centrally on the tanks whereas those on Nos 1–3 were located further forward. (Ron Copson, courtesy John Pigott)

**Walter Scott** was very much in vogue in the latter part of the nineteenth century and No. 6 *Peveril*, delivered from Beyer, Peacock in 1875, was named after a character in one of his novels, *Peveril of The Peak*, part of which takes place on the Island. It had its first replacement boiler in 1892, and then in 1911 was fitted with a new 3ft 3in-diameter boiler and enlarged water tanks. When another new boiler was fitted in 1932, the original Salter safety valves were replaced and its dome closed. Known as 'The Peel engine', *Peveril* was often out-shedded at Peel although it was latterly used as the Douglas Station pilot until its boiler finally expired in August 1960. After a period in store, it was repainted into the new Ailsa green livery and placed on static display at St John's in 1967, and at Douglas Station in 1973. After languishing for many years in the carriage shed, it is now on display in the IMR Museum at Port Erin, repainted by volunteers into the post-war Indian red livery.

(John McCann/Online Transport Archive)

**No. 7** *Tynwald* built by Beyer, Peacock in 1880, was withdrawn shortly before the Second World War and no colour images are known to exist. Its frames and bunker were plinthed for many years at Castletown Station, but are now in the UK.

**Sporting a** nameplate and an oval builder's plate on either side of the injector pipe, No. 8 was delivered from Beyer, Peacock in 1894 and named *Fenella* after the heroine in Walter Scott's novel *Peveril of the Peak*. After being given boilers from other engines in 1908 and 1915, it received a brand-new boiler in 1919. Then, in 1936, *Fenella* was fitted with a special one-off 2ft 10¾ in diameter boiler, closed dome and Ross 'Pop' safety valves. Although this was meant to supply the same tractive effort as the wider-diameter boilers fitted to Nos 4–6 and Nos 10–13, *Fenella* had a tendency to run short of steam when hauling heavy trains. After spending much of its active life on the northern services, sometimes out-shedded at Ramsey, No. 8 was withdrawn at the end of the 1968 season, by which time it was the last of the small-boilered engines still in use. The following year it was tested on the Port Erin line, but without success and subsequently languished in store until purchased for preservation by the Isle of Man Railway Society. When work began on restoring it to working order the boiler was sent for repair to the Severn Valley Railway. However, on return to the Island, the boiler was loaned to the IMR and fitted into No. 1 *Sutherland*, thus enabling the 1873 veteran to participate in the 1998 events marking the 125th anniversary of the opening of the Peel line. After three years, the boiler was finally transferred to *Fenella*, which allowed No. 8 to join the active fleet until 2008. The engine reverted to the ownership of the Railway in 2012 and is again in the operational fleet. (Les Folkard/Online Transport Archive)

**Named after** the Island's capital, No. 9 *Douglas* was another one-off from Beyer, Peacock (1896) and the last to be delivered with a small-diameter boiler. Like No. 8, its nameplates and builder's plates were positioned on either side of the injector pipe. In 1909, it was given the refurbished boiler from *Fenella;* then, in 1912, it was fitted with a brand new 3ft 3in diameter boiler and enlarged side tanks that survived until it was withdrawn in November 1953. Latterly, it spent most of its time as the Douglas Station pilot, and was photographed in this role in August 1953 still with its sloping smokebox and Salter safety valves. The Indian red livery, with the attractive black and yellow lining, was introduced in 1945. After a lengthy period in store, *Douglas* was cosmetically restored and occasionally displayed as a static exhibit. Although sold to the Isle of Man Railway Society in 1978, No. 9 has been stored on the railway since then, but is not on public display owing in part to asbestos contamination, a problem which also affects *Mona.* Today, No. 9 is of major historical significance as it is the only small-boilered locomotive still in virtually original condition. (Jim Jarvis/Kidderminster Railway Museum)

**In order** to haul heavier trains on the Ramsey line, the next four locomotives delivered from Beyer, Peacock between 1905 and 1908 were a little larger than their predecessors. They had medium-sized 3ft 3in boilers pressurised to 160psi, 480-gallon side tanks, Salter safety valves, bell mouth domes, higher cabs, centrally-positioned name plates and small oval builder's plates on the cab side, and were capable of working across the network. Following their delivery, Nos 1–9 were often assigned to the Peel/Ramsey services, although those engines later upgraded with larger boilers and side tanks did haul less heavy trains on the southern line. Proudly carrying the name of a former IMR director and Company secretary, George Henry Wood, No. 10 entered service as *G.H.Wood* in 1905. New boilers were fitted in 1926 and 1946, each having Ross 'Pop' safety valves and closed domes. This view taken at St John's on 2 September 1968 highlights the green livery introduced in 1967 with black and white lining, green driving wheels and, in this instance, red coupling rods. When its boiler failed in 1977, *G.H.Wood* was withdrawn and placed in store, until it was resuscitated and returned to service in 1993 with the refurbished boiler from No. 13. After an overhaul in 2006/7, the locomotive remains in service today, carrying the green livery of the Lord Ailsa years. (John McCann/Online Transport Archive)

**Delivered in** 1905, No. 11 also carried the name of one of the railway's directors, Dalrymple Maitland. New boilers with Ross 'Pop' safety valves and closed domes were fitted in 1934 and 1959. Renowned for its reliability, *Maitland* was one of the Island's stalwarts, first on the Ramsey line and then across the network. Note the Isle of Man Railway Company crest. In 1980, *Maitland* was given a new 3ft 7in diameter boiler supplied by Hunslet of Leeds. Stored since 2007, the locomotive is expected to return to service in the near future.
(Brian Faragher/Online Transport Archive)

**Named after** another IMR Company director, No. 12 *Hutchinson* arrived on the Island in 1908 and was noted for its distinctive, deeper tone whistle. Its original boiler, complete with closed dome and Salter safety valves, survived nearly 40 years until replaced by one from Beyer, Peacock in 1946. At the same time, a basic cast-iron chimney was fitted and small fleet numbers positioned above each nameplate. During its life, No. 12 spent much of its time on the southern line and was sometimes out-shedded at Port Erin. Like No. 11, it was in constant service, but by the late 1970s its boiler and water tanks were life-expired and it was withdrawn. During 1980 it was rebuilt with a new 3ft 7in diameter boiler supplied by Israel Newton. However, there were cries of outrage from traditionalists when it re-entered service with a square-shaped cab (similar to No. 16 *Mannin*) and in a blue livery. Its small tankside number plates had been removed, but these were reinstated when *Hutchinson* was again rebuilt during 1999/2000, this time with traditional-style cab and repainted in Indian red. These features are retained today, with *Hutchinson* being an important part of the active fleet.
(Phil Tatt/Online Transport Archive)

**No. 13** *Kissack* was delivered in 1910 and was a further locomotive named after an IMR board member. To keep it in service, No. 13 was given the refurbished boiler from No. 11 in 1944, followed five years later by the refurbished 1926 boiler from No. 10, at which point it lost its Salter safety valves. By the 1960s, this boiler was in poor shape so *Kissack* often appeared in the less strenuous role of Douglas Station pilot. In this view it was photographed at Ramsey in May 1959 double-heading a Douglas-bound train with No. 8 *Fenella*. *Kissack* was the only locomotive to have a brass cover round the Ross 'Pop' valves, although this was later transferred to No. 11. After many years in store, *Kissack* re-entered service in 1971 with a new boiler supplied by the Hunslet Engine Company of Leeds and, the following year, hauled a Royal Train from Castletown to Douglas. Together with *Loch,* it assumed responsibility for maintaining the basic service until withdrawn in 1991, its refurbished boiler being fitted into *G.H.Wood* in 1993. After another spell in store, *Kissack* eventually returned to traffic in 2006 and today forms part of the operational fleet. (G. W. Morant/Online Transport Archive)

**Following the** takeover of the Manx Northern Railway (MNR) in 1905, two of its four locomotives, No. 1 *Ramsey* and No. 2 *Northern*, were never renumbered into the IMR fleet and both were scrapped by the mid-1920s. Of the two locomotives to be renumbered, No. 3 *Thornhill* was built by Beyer, Peacock in 1880 and was similar to IMR engines Nos 1–3. It was named after the residence once occupied by the MNR Chairman. Numbered 14 by the IMR, *Thornhill* worked principally on the northern lines, often being out-shedded at Ramsey where this broadside portrait was taken on 26 May 1958. All the Island locomotives had cab-side canvases. Known as 'draught dodgers', these were fitted to both sides of the cab, and were meant to provide the crew with some protection from the torrential rain and fearsome gales that can buffet the island. When not in use the canvases were tucked into the cab side handrail as seen here. When withdrawn with a boiler defect in July 1963, *Thornhill* was still in virtually original condition complete with bell-mouth dome, Salter safety valves, sloping smokebox and 3ft 3in diameter boiler. Although still on the Island, it has been in private hands since 1978 and not on public view. (Charles Firminger, courtesy Bob Bridger)

**The other** MNR locomotive taken over in 1905 was No. 4 *Caledonia,* which had been built by Dübs and Co of Glasgow in 1885, the name reflecting its country of origin. This was an 0-6-0 tank engine which had been purchased to haul the heavy mineral trains over the short Foxdale Railway with its maximum grade of 1:49. As such, it was the most powerful engine on the Island. However, after being taken over by the IMR and renumbered No. 15, it saw infrequent use owing to its long rigid wheelbase which caused problems on some of the sharper curves. Despite these limitations, *Caledonia* was fitted with a new boiler and side tanks in 1922 as well as Ross 'Pop' safety valves. Until 1965, it served as the IMR snowplough and was photographed as such at Douglas in May 1951. Occasionally, it also hauled heavy cattle or engineering trains. (W. J. Wyse/LRTA (London Area)/ Online Transport Archive)

**After leading** a very quiet life for many years, No. 15 came out of 'retirement' in 1967 in order to overcome a chronic shortage of motive power and was returned to traffic painted in the new Ailsa green livery seen here. The following year, it aroused considerable interest when it was repainted in an approximation of its original MNR Tuscan red. After being taken out of traffic, 'Caley' was put on static display at St John's and Douglas before going to the new Port Erin Museum in 1975. Then in 1993 it was extracted from the Museum and, restored to working order so it could play a major role in the 1995 celebrations marking the centenary of the Snaefell Mountain Railway, to which the locomotive had been leased during the line's construction. After appearing for a time in a blue livery, it reverted to Tuscan red in 2007 and since 2014 it has been undergoing an overhaul. (Charles Firminger, courtesy Bob Bridger)

**The last** locomotive to be acquired by the IMR was No. 16 *Mannin*. Built by Beyer, Peacock and delivered in 1926, it was the most powerful of the 2-4-0 tank engines. Fitted with a 3ft 6in diameter boiler pressurised to 180psi and side tanks with a capacity of 520 gallons, it was able to haul the heaviest trains on the southern line without assistance, thereby eliminating the need for a second engine. *Mannin* was also noted for its shorter chimney, squat dome and more conventional square-shaped cab. However, like Nos 10–13, it had a centrally-positioned nameplate and a small oval builder's plate on the upper cab side. No. 16 spent nearly all its working life on the Port Erin line and was often out-shedded there. However, by the early 1960s, the locomotive's boiler was in poor condition so the engine was relegated to the relatively flat Douglas–Peel line until withdrawn in 1964. There is no record of this locomotive ever working beyond Kirk Michael towards Ramsey. After being repainted into Ailsa green for static display, *Mannin* appeared at St John's and Douglas until becoming a permanent exhibit at the Railway Museum in Port Erin in 1975 where it can still be seen today. (Phil Tatt/Online Transport Archive)

**To help** reduce costs and provide much-needed cover for the increasingly vulnerable steam locomotives, especially during the winter months, the IMR purchased two single-ended railcars from the County Donegal Railways Joint Committee on 1 March 1961. Dating from 1950 (No. 19) and 1951 (No. 20), the cabs on these articulated units were built by Walker Bros of Wigan and the 41-seat carriage bodies by the Great Northern Railway of Ireland at their Dundalk Works, power being supplied by reliable Gardner 6LW diesel engines. Retaining their County Donegal fleet numbers, Nos 19 and 20 were coupled back to back by the IMR, and were used initially to cover the sparse winter timetable. Then, from 1962, they worked mostly on the Peel line as well as between St John's and Kirk Michael. They did venture onto the southern line despite encountering power problems on the steep climb out of Douglas. This view shows the pair shortly after arrival in August 1962. After closure of the northern lines, both remained available for service until relegated to works duties in 1975, but their use was infrequent. The railway began a major rebuild of the railcars in the late 1990s and much work was completed, including new body framing, seat retrimming and reconditioning of the Gardner engines. However, the project ran significantly over-budget and was suspended by an incoming management, but work has recently recommenced. (Brian Faragher/Online Transport Archive)

**Coverage of** the rail network begins at Douglas. The original wooden-framed station, which was built in 1873 for the opening of the Peel line, soon proved inadequate as the system expanded, so the area was redesigned to include new station buildings, an office block, a six-track station with two island platforms, locomotive shed and works, a carriage storage shed as well as a goods depot and sidings. Built with Ruabon red brick, the station was completed in time for the 1892 season. This view shows the entrance added in 1899 with its wide brick arch, above which is a clock and the words 'Railway Station' flanked by two gilded domes. In 1960, the popular weekly Holiday Run-About Ticket cost 10/- (50p), about half a week's wage for the average person.
(Phil Tatt/Online Transport Archive)

**By July** 1964, the price of the weekly Run-About Ticket had risen by fifty per cent to 15/- (75p). This scene shows the railway administrative block now occupied in part by the Customs & Excise Department, whilst the road on the left leads to the goods yard, cattle sidings and warehouse accommodation. Of particular interest is the billboard advertising the Sunday morning church trains to Kirk Braddan at a return fare of 1/- (5p). (Marcus Eavis/Online Transport Archive)

**This busy** station was the nerve centre of the Island's railways. To provide cover on the exposed platforms, attractive canopies were erected in 1909 and the booking hall was extended to incorporate the former open concourse. As the largest and busiest narrow-gauge station in the British Isles, it rapidly became a magnet for visitors and enthusiasts, one of whom, John McCann, captured No. 3 *Pender* moving onto the engine release road after uncoupling from its train on 1 August 1953. This magnificent photograph shows part of the platform canopies, the grand high-level entrance with its glided domes and the track-side floral displays, complete with palm trees. (John McCann/Online Transport Archive)

**In another** view taken in early August 1953, this time on a somewhat overcast day, No. 14 *Thornhill* was at the head of a train on number two road whilst station pilot No. 9 *Douglas* was occupying number four road. A few months after this view was taken, *Douglas* was taken out of service, making it the third Beyer, Peacock to be withdrawn. (Jim Jarvis/Kidderminster Railway Museum)

**On 23** August 1953, No. 6 *Peveril* prepares to depart for Peel. Normally, two carriages were sufficient for through trains on each of the northern lines, except for school workings and at times of peak seasonal demand. (John McCann/Online Transport Archive)

**At certain** times of the day the commodious waiting room, attractive cafe, booking hall, concourse and platforms bustled with activity, but for most of the time the station was a haven of tranquillity except for the occasional locomotive movement. In this charming study, No. 8 *Fenella* shunts an open wagon and a rake of four carriages headed by F21 on 6 September 1963. Railway rolling stock was categorised according to a letter classification, with the F-series covering bogie passenger-carrying vehicles introduced between 1876 and 1926. Seventy-eight small 'Two-Plank Wagons' constituted the M-series, one of which can be seen between the locomotive and the passenger coaches. Built between 1877 and 1926, the M-series had fully drop-down sides. No. 8 may have been assembling the stock for the afternoon school train to Peel.
(Brian Faragher/Online Transport Archive)

**Sitting beside** his granddad on the Peel arrival platform, a little lad waves to No. 10 *G.H.Wood* as it leaves with the 3.40pm to Port Erin on 18 July 1964. For almost the entire history of the line, locomotives have all faced the same way, and hence the vast majority of departures from Douglas were chimney-first and arrivals bunker-first. (Marcus Eavis/Online Transport Archive)

**Over the** years, Douglas Station was developed and upgraded. Although the iron-framed canopies were a much-admired feature, they suffered badly from corrosion. When it was decided to reduce the station facilities as part of a major rationalisation programme, work began on removing them in 1979. Somehow their disappearance seemed to symbolise the changing face of the railway. The general air of neglect has been captured in this view of No. 4 *Loch* waiting to depart from the canopy-less platform at the head of *'The Viking'*.

(John L. May/Online Transport Archive)

**When exploring** the Station, it was not only the locomotives which attracted attention, but also the different types of carriages. Until the late 1950s, as many as seventy from a total fleet of seventy-five could be required at the height of the season. To cope with increased traffic on the expanding network by the mid-1870s, fifty-six four-wheel carriages built by the Metropolitan Carriage & Wagon Co. (MC&W) were in operation. Between 1909 and 1926 the bodies from some of these were joined together and mounted on new bogie frames supplied by MC&W to create a single unit known as 'Pairs'. These were especially useful at times of peak summer demand or on Tynwald Fair Day when thousands flocked to St John's. 'Pairs' were also regularly used for school workings on the Peel line until the 1950s. Painted in two shades of brown, F72 is seen on 1 August 1953 at the west end of the long carriage shed situated on the south side of the station complex. This 'Pair' comprised an original, all first-class, three-compartment body joined to an unusual first and third three-compartment composite. In 1967, the bodies from eleven 'Pairs' were scrapped and the bogie frames, renumbered in a new R-series, used for a short time to transport containers. In 1974, the frames were sold to the Ffestiniog Railway. Some 'Pairs' survive on the Island, but just two (F54 and F62) in the operational fleet.

(John McCann/Online Transport Archive)

**Often a** long rake of carriages was parked on number one road, the northernmost track in the Station. At the head of this line-up, taken in May 1961, is F5, one of the first group of six wooden-bodied 40-seat bogie carriages (F1–F6) built by Brown Marshalls & Co and delivered in 1876 with twin running boards on each side. During the next eighteen years, thirteen similar 'Small Fs' were delivered – F7 and F8 by the Ashbury Carriage & Wagon Co, and F9–F19 by Brown Marshalls. Only six 'Small Fs' remain in stock today. This view shows the guard's handbrake projecting from the back of F5, which was scrapped in 1976. (Phil Tatt/Online Transport Archive)

**Wooden-bodied F31** of 1905 represents the first saloon carriages supplied by MC&W, which had absorbed Brown Marshalls in 1902. These improved vehicles did not have footboards. Seen in the bright post-war red and cream livery on 18 July 1964, this vehicle now forms part of the popular 'bar set'. (Marcus Eavis/Online Transport Archive)

**Another interesting** vehicle to be found on site was Morris Commercial No. 6, used by the Railway Permanent Way Department. It was imported to the Island having previously been used by GPO Telephones. By the time of this picture in June 1973, it was dumped, awaiting disposal. (Brian Faragher/Online Transport Archive)

**Sometimes photographers** were lucky and succeeded in recording freight movements within the Station complex. On 3 August 1953, No. 10 *G.H.Wood* is shown here moving six four-wheel cattle wagons, including K13, from the rear of a mixed train from Ramsey. In all probability, the animals would have been acquired at the town's cattle market. Once the cattle had been off-loaded, the wagons would be taken to the washing siding located near the back of the carriage shed where they would be thoroughly cleaned and disinfected. The K-series were built between 1873 and 1924, and the last were scrapped in 1965. Very few colour images exist of these cattle wagons in use. (John McCann/Online Transport Archive)

**Whilst making** his way to the signal box on 1 August 1953, John McCann took this view of No. 12 *Hutchinson*. Although there was at least one passenger on board and the signal was set for a departure, John's notes state 'shunting at Douglas'.
(John McCann/Online Transport Archive)

**On 3** August 1953, No. 14 *Thornhill* was in charge of a five-carriage departure for Ramsey. The leading bogie coach F3 was one of the original batch of 'Small Fs' delivered in 1876. Note the group of H-series four-wheel wagons, these particular examples having additional high-sided rails for the movement of cattle. Delivered between 1873 and 1925, this series of forty-nine 'Three-Plank Wagons', with their drop-down centre doors, were the mainstay of freight operations for many years.
(John McCann/Online Transport Archive)

**Both these** scenes were recorded on 3 August 1953. In the first, No. 16 *Mannin* was departing at the start of its journey to Port Erin. This was the locomotive which had been specifically purchased to work the heaviest trains on the busy southern line. To the right were additional carriage sidings, and on the far right the goods shed and yard where No. 10 *G.H.Wood* was assembling a mixed train of goods vehicles. In the second view, taken a few minutes later, No. 1 *Sutherland* passes the locomotive works with a train from Ramsey whilst No. 10 simmers quietly in the foreground, waiting to continue its shunting operations. (John McCann/Online Transport Archive (both))

**As illustrated** earlier, the coaling area was ideal for taking portrait shots of the engines. Looking particularly resplendent on 1 August 1953, No. 12 *Hutchinson* and No. 3 *Pender* have just taken on water during one of the quick between-duties turnrounds dictated by the timetable and are now in the queue to be recoaled. (John McCann/Online Transport Archive)

**A short** time after the last view was taken, *Pender* has arrived at the coaling platform with the ready-filled wire or wicker panniers. Following the opening of the line to Ramsey and the branch down to the harbour, coal from Britain was transferred directly from ship to train and then transported to the various locomotive sheds. However, by the early 1950s, transfers were undertaken by lorry. In order to have sufficient supplies for the summer schedule, significant stockpiles were assembled at each running shed, especially Douglas, where stacks of coal could be found at several places, an elderly Priestman crane being used to make the transfers to the refuelling point. (John McCann/Online Transport Archive)

**Another major** source of interest was the locomotive shed, which was especially busy when the shed staff and locomotive crews were either raising steam for the day ahead or damping down the fires and raking out the ash, prior to bedding down for the night. There were also periods of intense activity during the working day when the locomotives were carefully checked between duties. On 18 June 1960, the shed is empty, but No. 14 *Thornhill* and No. 11 *Maitland* are in steam outside whilst No12 *Hutchinson* is being coaled and watered, No. 5 *Mona* is taking water on an adjacent track and No. 13 *Kissack* is probably acting as Station pilot. Five locomotives in steam in one photograph – quite a coup. This was the entire complement of locomotives operated from Douglas Shed that year. (Les Folkard/Online Transport Archive)

**This overview** of the Station throat taken on 1 August 1953 provides a good impression of the sprawl of land owned by the railway. From left to right are the workshops with the two large, roof-mounted water tanks, an array of signals including the elegant home signals in the foreground, the signal box and the long, somewhat rudimentary, carriage shed. All the signalling in this area was installed by Dutton & Co. of Worcester. (John McCann/Online Transport Archive)

**An organised** visit to the engine shed and workshops was always a highlight for any visiting enthusiast. No one quite knew what they would find. As passenger numbers declined and investment dwindled, it was here that skilled staff battled to keep the increasingly elderly locomotives operational. As detailed earlier, some were withdrawn with life-expired boilers whilst others could be laid up for many years with a view to possible repair at some point. This whole area was a functioning timewarp. After being stored for several years, No. 4 *Loch* was rehabilitated during 1968 and fitted with a new boiler. It is seen in the workshop on 1 September just days before undergoing steam trials. The new spring-green livery had been introduced in 1967 by the Marquess of Ailsa when he took out a twenty-one-year lease on the railway with a five-year get-out clause. After entering service in early September 1968, No. 4 did work a few passenger trains on the northern lines, but as the mounting losses were clearly unsustainable, the Peel and Ramsey lines closed for passengers at the end of the 1968 season. However, for a few more months, No. 4 often hauled the handful of oil trains between Peel and Ramsey until these movements ended on 29 April 1969. They had only started on 13 August 1968! (John McCann/Online Transport Archive)

**This view** taken in August 1979 shows much of the vintage, belt-driven machinery and the small overhead crane which was capable of lifting up to 10 tons. Space was cramped and the working area restricted. At this time, No. 12 *Hutchinson* was undergoing the major rebuild described earlier, complete with square-type cab and blue livery. (G. W. Price)

**There now** follows a group of photographs taken at different times between 1953 and 1968. They follow the course of the original 11½ mile IMR line to Peel and the 16½ mile MNR line from St John's to Ramsey, which opened in 1879 and was absorbed by the IMR in 1905. This scene, taken on 2 August 1953, shows No. 10 *G.H.Wood* inbound for Douglas with a two-coach train from Ramsey on the open section north of Quarter Bridge. (John McCann/Online Transport Archive)

**Seen on** the same section as the previous view, the ex-County Donegal railcars are working the 2.10pm departure from Douglas to Kirk Michael on 2 August 1966. In fine weather, the handful of Ramsey trains were usually well-filled, especially by people making for the popular pleasure grounds at Glen Wyllin, located near Kirk Michael Station. It is interesting to note the different variations of livery carried by the railcars during the years covered by this book, especially around the front grilles. (Charles Firminger, courtesy Bob Bridger)

**Here, No.** 12 *Hutchinson* crosses the Castletown road near Quarter Bridge on 13 August 1967. This was the site of a short-lived halt which for a brief period during 1928/9 was used by people travelling to view the Island's famous motorcycle races.
(Alan Murray-Rust/Online Transport Archive)

**An unusual** operation on this section of line centred around the halt at Braddan. Opened in 1897, it was only used on Sunday mornings during the high summer when hundreds of worshippers made the 1½ mile journey from Douglas so that they could attend the well-publicised open-air services at Kirk Braddan Parish Church. Fortunately, John McCann was on hand to photograph these 'specials' on Sunday, 2 August 1953. Although there were two official departures from Douglas at 10.10am and 10.40am, John's notes record that three train loads were carried that day, hauled by No. 4 *Loch* and No. 10 *G.H.Wood*. After unloading its passengers, No. 4 prepares to leave Braddan for Union Mills.

(John McCann/Online Transport Archive)

**As there** were no run-round facilities at Braddan, the empty stock had to be taken a mile up the line to Union Mills where the locomotive could use the passing loop. After it had completed this manoeuvre, John obtained this remarkable view of No. 10 hauling sixteen carriages back towards Douglas. On one occasion a total of eighteen carriages were recorded.

(John McCann/Online Transport Archive)

**Some time** later, No. 4 was back at Braddan, reputedly with the third train from Douglas. After alighting, people reached the open-air service by walking up a flight of steps onto the main road. When these views were taken, the 'church specials' were the only trains using the northern lines on Sunday.

(John McCann/Online Transport Archive

**In this** view taken from the road bridge, No. 10 *G.H.Wood* is at the head of a rake of smart-looking saloon coaches, all of which were painted brown and cream. In the distance, No. 4 *Loch* is waiting with another train as there were two scheduled return journeys, at 11.50am and 12 noon. During the duration of the service, footplate crews were under strict instructions not to sound their whistles or to let off steam. Note the absence of any platform as well as the staff gathered near the small wooden waiting shelter – hardly ideal should the heavens open, which they often do. (John McCann/Online Transport Archive)

**These church** specials were revived during the summers of 1967 and 1968, although loadings were much reduced as people had found alternative means of transport. On 28 August 1967, No. 5 *Mona* is waiting with just three carriages to carry the small number of worshippers booked to return to Douglas. Some time later, the small wooden waiting room was uplifted and relocated to Colby on the south line.

(Charles Firminger, courtesy Bob Bridger)

**The next** station was Union Mills, located 2½ miles from Douglas. Although officially closed in November 1954, it was almost certainly used the following summer. For many years, it had been famous for its magnificent floral displays, but these had long gone when the Station was reopened by the new Ailsa management on 3 June 1967. Although a platform existed on the down track, trains in both directions now used the former eastbound track. However, the passing loop continued to be used by the Braddan church trains. Just days before final closure, a down train waits to depart for St John's on 31 August 1968.
(John McCann/Online Transport Archive)

**At the** start of the 1968 season, No. 5 *Mona* was photographed leaving Crosby on 3 June with a Peel to Douglas train consisting of half-luggage carriage F40 of 1907, the body of which was scrapped in 1977 and the frames in 2011. Located some 4½ miles from Douglas, the Station at Crosby was latterly run down and little used. (Bernard Harrison, courtesy Bob Bridger)

**Near the** end of the 1968 season, a down train approaches Crosby on 31 August. The brick and timber building visible on the up side had a booking office, waiting rooms, including one for ladies only, and a porter's room. There were also two sidings leading off the up track serving a cattle dock and a small goods shed. However, by this time, all freight operation had ended, although Crosby could still be used as a crossing point. (John McCann/Online Transport Archive)

**For much** of its length the IMR followed the course of the River Dhoo through the central valley between the mountains. This rural scene was photographed from a spot on the main A1 road at Greeba, close to the *'Highlander'*, a former coaching inn. No. 5 *Mona* is shown chugging along the valley bottom on 28 August 1967 with the 3.40pm from Douglas to Peel. (Charles Firminger, courtesy Bob Bridger)

**Located 8½** miles from Douglas, the junction at St John's became a hive of activity a few times a day when trains from Douglas, Peel and Ramsey were often divided and reassembled. According to demand, a service could consist of anything from one to ten carriages, although trains with more than eight were rare. Sometimes trains were double-headed, usually to enable the second engine to return to base. This pair was photographed storming towards Douglas on 31 August 1968. (John McCann/Online Transport Archive)

**Fifteen years** earlier, on 1 August 1953, the same photographer stood on the high bridge carrying the Foxdale branch over the main line so he could take this enchanting view of No. 8 *Fenella*, which has stopped short of St John's so that the guard can uncouple the rear two carriages. This allows the locomotive to then proceed with the front two which it will take on to Peel. Another locomotive will soon back down and couple up to the Ramsey portion. On the right was the overgrown siding serving the ballast crushing plant. (John McCann/Online Transport Archive)

**The previous** photograph was taken from the high stone arch seen in this view taken on 2 June 1968. St John's had been the junction for the steeply-graded Foxdale Railway, built to transport ore from the lead mines. This traffic had ceased by 1911 and thereafter the passenger service, consisting of four return journeys, staggered on until replaced by buses in 1940. However, the branch did see increased activity between 1936 and 1943 when spoil from the mines was taken by No. 15 *Caledonia* for use in the construction of two RAF airfields. Once this traffic ended, the by-now infrequent goods service finally closed. The large tank (left) gathered water from the Foxdale alignment and was used to supplement the tanks at St John's. To the left of the running line was the start of the siding serving the former large ballast pit.

(Ron Copson, courtesy John Pigott)

**Many enthusiasts** would often take time to explore the Foxdale branch, sometimes by walking the full 2½ miles. The last trains had operated over the branch in January 1960 and the first view was taken in early 1962 when much of the track was still present. The second view dates from 8 September 1967, by which time much of the site had been partially cleared and any remaining rolling stock removed. Some track was still in situ in the 1970s.

(Brian Faragher/Online Transport Archive: John McCann/Online Transport Archive)

**With the** Foxdale Bridge forming the backdrop, light engine No. 10 *G.H.Wood* has the down home signal to proceed into St John's Station on 2 June 1968. The building on the left was part of the substantial carriage shed. (John McCann/Online Transport Archive)

**In this** view, No. 10 G.H.Wood is assembling a train of mixed stock to form the 4.41pm from St John's to Douglas on 1 August 1953. The four-wheel G-series van nearest the camera, G14, was built by the IMR in 1897 whilst G8 was built the same year, but by MC&W. After being out of use for several years, both were scrapped in 1975. (John McCann/Online Transport Archive)

**The Island** had only two signal boxes – at Douglas and St John's. The latter, constructed of stone and wood, was paid for by the MNR, but located on the north side of the IMR main line. With the increase in traffic following the opening of the Ramsey line, it controlled all movements in and around the much-expanded junction.

(John McCann/Online Transport Archive)

**Sometimes referred** to as the Manx equivalent of Crewe or Clapham Junction, St John's Station had three open platforms. On the south side was a single platform which also housed the substantial station building, whilst on the north side was an island platform. During the few spells of intense weekday activity, the sidings on the north side were sometimes used as well. This next sequence, taken between 2.32pm and 2.38pm on 1 August 1953, captures something of the organised hustle and bustle. At 2.32pm, No. 1 *Sutherland* has uncoupled from the carriages it has just brought in from Ramsey whilst, in the background, No. 8 *Fenella* will eventually take the carriages from Peel and Ramsey into Douglas.

(John McCann/Online Transport Archive)

**In the** second view taken at 2.33pm, No. 4 *Loch* has just arrived at the Peel platform with the 2.10pm from Douglas, the carriages for Ramsey having been uncoupled just short of the signal box.

(John McCann/Online Transport Archive)

**In the** third view, No. 8 is on the north side of the island platform, having coupled up to the carriages from Ramsey and Peel in order to form the 2.37pm departure for Douglas.
(John McCann/Online Transport Archive)

**In the** fourth view, No. 1 is ready to depart for Ramsey at 2.38pm. In the background is F39. Known as the *'Foxdale Coach'*, owing to its long association with the branch, it was built by the Bristol & South Wales Carriage Co and still forms part of today's fleet, having recently been splendidly restored to original condition.
(John McCann/Online Transport Archive)

**Once peace** descended, there was always plenty to see whilst waiting for the next burst of activity, although by August 1961 any remaining goods traffic was mostly carried by railway-owned lorries. The Station yard and sidings looked neglected, the enamel signs were rusty, and the adverts were peeling and faded. These advertisements had once provided a much-needed source of additional revenue for the railway. Waiting to be photographed during the lull in proceedings is an unidentified G-series closed van and M49, an open wagon built by MC&W in 1911. The railway had carried nearly 50,000 tons of freight a year in the 1930s, and even as late as 1955 it was still handling some 12,000 tons. This consisted of fish, iron, timber, flour, grain, hay, straw, tar, milk, livestock, beer and spirits, vegetables and potatoes plus all manner of other consignments. However, competing road hauliers continued to eat into the railway's freight business and it declined further. Parts of St John's Station site are now occupied by a primary school and a car park across the road from the *Farmer's Arms* in Station Road.

(Phil Tatt/Online Transport Archive)

**Some of** the many redundant carriages stored at St John's had been in the open for many years. Of particular interest were the former MNR six-wheelers which had not been used for quite some time, probably since the 1930s. Mounted on Cleminson flexible underframes, they were 5ft shorter than the 'Small Fs' and had six-door bodies built by Swansea Carriage & Wagon Co. with one set of running boards on each side. Of the original fourteen, twelve passed to the IMR in 1905 and were numbered N40–N51. Looking in reasonably good condition, this unidentified example was photographed on 27 May 1959. It was during this visit that the photographer was told by the station master that these 'Cleminsons' had been used into the 1950s on excursion trains, but no evidence has ever come to light. (Marcus Eavis/Online Transport Archive)

**Included in** this line, quietly mouldering alongside the carriage shed in August 1961, is another group of 'Cleminsons', including N50. In 1964, N41 became a mess hut outside Douglas Locomotive Shed and, in 1975, N42 was purchased privately for preservation and fully restored. Displayed for some time in the Port Erin Railway Museum, it was transferred to the UK in 2013. A turntable was installed at St John's in the mid-1920s and, although this was used to turn locomotives, it was also used to reduce the paint bill by turning the carriages stored in the open to ensure they were weathered uniformly on both sides.
(Phil Tatt/Online Transport Archive)

**Following the** closure of the northern lines, carriages continued to be moved to and from storage at St John's along the rusty, weed-strewn track until the early 1970s. Unfortunately, the site was no longer staffed and the carriage shed, which had been built in 1905, was subjected to break-ins and vandalism. This view of the semi-derelict interior was taken on 8 June 1975, just months before the building was virtually destroyed by an arson attack in December, as a result of which the last of the original wooden-bodied carriages (F1–F6) and the last Ashbury (F7) were deemed to be beyond rescue. This was particularly depressing as some had just been earmarked for preservation. F17 (right) was burned by the scrapmen in November. (G. W. Price)

**Often parked** at St John's were F27 and F28, the two 'Empress Vans', so named because they were delivered from MC&W in 1897, the year of Queen Victoria's Diamond Jubilee. Used for transporting luggage and parcels, they also served as ambulance units during the TT races and the Manx Grand Prix. Both were withdrawn in 1992. No. 27 was photographed here outside the carriage shed in August 1961. It survived until 2012 when its body was scrapped, although the frames remain in store. (Phil Tatt/Online Transport Archive)

**Parked on** the north side of the Station in the summer of 1963 are the railcars. Later, they would proceed to Kirk Michael to work an afternoon departure to Douglas. Following their acquisition in 1961, the railcars maintained the sparse winter timetable which comprised a couple of return trips to Port Erin interspersed with one to Peel, basically for the movement of parcels and light goods. In the background was one of the 'Empress Vans'. (E. J. McWatt/ Online Transport Archive)

**To attract** more visitors, several stored locomotives were put on display during the 1968 season, but each evening they were shunted back into the relative security of the carriage shed. Photographed on 28 August 1968 from left to right are Nos 15, 16, 6, 1 and 14. In 1967, No. 15 *Caledonia* had been returned to steam and painted in Ailsa green, but, for this season, it carried the MNR Tuscan red livery (seen here) as well as its original MNR number 4. (John McCann/Online Transport Archive)

**On 2** June 1968, *'Caley'* hauled a well-filled special organised by the IOM Steam Railway Supporters Association, which is seen here shortly after arrival at St John's, having stopped at the Peel platform. The leading carriage is F75, the last of the 'Pairs' to enter service in 1926, and which is now on display at the Isle of Man Railway Museum. (Bernard Harrison, courtesy Bob Bridger)

**In 1968**, a contract was secured to move oil from the Electricity Board Plant at Peel to a power station at Ramsey, special sidings being laid at both locations. To carry the oil, the IMR workshop staff created three new vehicles using the frames from M-series wagons. The first movement was on 13 August 1968. On arrival at St John's, the tankers had to be shunted in order to be attached to the rear of a passenger train. Here, No. 10 *G.H.Wood* undertakes this manoeuvre on 2 September 1968. Note the different size tanks and the crude wooden supports. When these oil trains were discontinued at the end of April 1969, all rail operation beyond St John's to Peel and Ramsey finally came to an end.
(Charles Firminger, courtesy Bob Bridger)

**This next** group of photographs covers the 3-mile section from St John's to Peel. For a short distance after leaving St John's, the MNR track (left) and the IMR track to Peel (right) ran parallel for about half a mile. Overlooked by Tynwald Hill, No. 4 *Loch* makes a spirited departure for Peel with the 2.36pm from St John's on 1 August 1953 and has just crossed the level crossing on the west side of the Station.
(John McCann/Online Transport Archive)

**With the** IOM and MNR lines running side by side on the west side of St John's it was possible to photograph trains on both sections sometimes steaming neck and neck, often with the Peel train slightly ahead as seen on 23 May 1959. For the next three miles the Peel line followed the course of the River Neb. (Marcus Eavis/Online Transport Archive)

**The simultaneous** departures also enabled one train to be photographed from the other – for example, this view of Peel-bound No. 10 *G.H.Wood* was taken from a Ramsey train in August 1967. (Alan Murray-Rust/Online Transport Archive)

**Situated alongside** the harbour, the terminal facilities at Peel were quite extensive, with an island platform, and a substantial Station building complete with canopy, goods sidings, raised cattle dock and locomotive shed. On 23 May 1959, No. 12 *Hutchinson* has just arrived with two coaches, the leading one, F13, dating from 1894. On the opposite side of the island platform stands a train of 'Pairs', including F51 of 1912. Painted in overall chocolate brown, these are probably waiting to work the late-afternoon school train to Douglas. At the end of the platform is an IMR lorry. (Marcus Eavis/Online Transport Archive)

**With the** harbour and castle forming a backdrop, No. 8 *Fenella* runs back to take on coal and water in September 1967.
(Brian Faragher/Online Transport Archive)

**In July** 1956, No. 10 *G.H.Wood* stands alongside the water tower. In the foreground is the crew rest room and in the background the Mill Road level crossing through which the trains pass in order to access the Station complex. The small engine shed is on the right. Today, the Station building and water tower still stand, together with a short section of track, as reminders of the former line which closed to passengers on 7 September 1968 and goods on 29 April 1969. During the early 1960s, the number of trains had been reduced and it did seem as if the railway might be shut down for good when the IMR announced on 13 November 1965 that the whole network was closing immediately to allow 'essential maintenance to take place'. As a result, no passenger trains were operated at all during 1966 and it was only when the Marquess of Ailsa acquired the lease that the railway reopened for the 1967 season, the timetable including a limited weekday service to Peel. A small transport museum has been established in the former brickworks office across the road from the water tower and rail display.
(John McCann/Online Transport Archive)

**The 16½-mile** line between St John's and Ramsey was opened by the MNR in 1879. Although relations with the IMR were strained, some through carriages were operated into Douglas. As already illustrated, the IMR and MNR lines ran parallel for about half a mile after leaving St John's. In this view taken on 1 August 1953, No. 1 *Sutherland* is in charge of the 2.38pm to Ramsey, the first carriage being F21. (John McCann/Online Transport Archive)

**In contrast** to the virtually flat Douglas–Peel line, the MNR was heavily engineered. On leaving St John's the line veered northwards on a long sweeping embankment. No. 8 *Fenella* has just crossed the main A1 Douglas–Ramsey road on 19 August 1960 with a two-coach train heading towards St Germain's.

(Les Folkard/Online Transport Archive)

**Double-headed by** No. 10 *G.H.Wood* and No. 8 *Fenella*, this well-loaded train is making for St John's in July 1956. The front carriage was one of the 'Pairs', probably added to the formation to provide much-needed additional capacity.

(John McCann/Online Transport Archive)

**The Ramsey** line mostly served isolated farming communities scattered along the north-west coast, and this view of St Germain's taken on 1 August 1953 captures much of the charm of a typical narrow-gauge rural railway. As this was officially a 'request stop', a red flag was displayed to inform the driver that he needed to stop for intending passengers or to collect goods such as the milk churns seen on the trackside. Lack of passengers led to closure of the station in July 1961, although trains would continue to stop if pre-arranged with the crew. From the outset, St Germain's had a passing loop which, after a period of closure, was reinstated in 1926. Unlike the more utilitarian structures on the IMR, the MNR built substantial sandstone stations with tall chimneys, double gables and slate roofs, this one surviving today as a private residence. As with St John's, the apostrophe in St Germain's could be omitted on tickets, and from timetables and advertising literature.

(John McCann/Online Transport Archive)

**Long-standing friends,** John McCann and Jim Jarvis were both keen railway photographers and early users of colour slides. On 1 August 1953 they spent the day photographing together, often standing literally side by side. However, at St Germain's, John took the view on the previous page whilst Jim waited a little longer so he could feature more of No. 1 *Sutherland,* but, in doing so, he also managed to include John who can be seen just in front of the locomotive, looking particularly smart for a day of steam, soot and sparks. Between them the two enthusiasts made an invaluable record of the IMR, mostly in glorious weather, over sixty years ago. (Jim Jarvis/Kidderminster Railway Museum)

**A particularly** scenic section existed around Gob-y-Deigan where the single-track line had been built on an exposed shelf cut into the rocks overlooking the Irish Sea. Known as 'Donkey Bank', this stretch proved liable to subsidence and coastal erosion and, over many years, time and money was spent trying to prevent the track from being destroyed. The platelayer's hut on the left side would have provided a degree of shelter for men working on the line during these periods. During the Island's frequent spells of inclement weather, this isolated section was a real challenge for the driver and fireman as the little locomotives battled against the elements. However, on 1 August 1953, No. 8 *Fenella* is bathed in sunshine as it snakes towards St Germain's with a train from Ramsey consisting of two small F-series carriages and a G-series van. (John McCann/Online Transport Archive)

**With Peel** visible on the horizon, No. 10 *G.H.Wood* steams through the rugged coastal scenery with the 10.47am St John's to Ramsey on 3 June 1968. Those on board could not have known this would be the line's last year of operation. Although the Marquess of Ailsa had reintroduced the service to Ramsey, passenger loadings were generally disappointing. Few local people now used the railway so revenue was derived almost entirely from tourists and enthusiasts. To help reduce costs, trains were restricted to Monday, Wednesdays and Fridays during the summer seasons of 1967/68. In times past, a short-lived halt had existed near this spot. (Bernard Harrison, courtesy Bob Bridger)

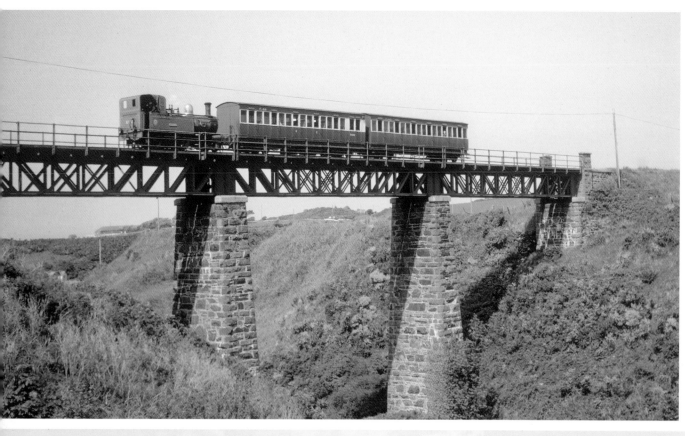

**The MNR** built two substantial viaducts spanning deep glens, each of which featured towering stone pillars. The original bridge at Glen Mooar was replaced in 1921 by the structure shown here on Whit Monday, 3 June 1968, with No. 10 *G.H.Wood* heading towards St John's. (Bernard Harrison, courtesy Bob Bridger)

**On 31** August 1968, a mixed train crosses the viaduct. At the rear are the three oil tankers carrying fuel for the power station at Ramsey. (Charles Firminger, courtesy Bob Bridger)

**The second** viaduct just south of Kirk Michael spanned Glen Wyllin where the original MNR bridge was replaced in 1915. During the late Victorian period, the Glen was developed into a popular destination for residents and visitors. The railcars are shown crossing the viaduct on 3 August 1964. After the line closed, both viaducts were dismantled, although the stone supports were left in place, gaunt reminders of a bygone age. (Charles Firminger, courtesy Bob Bridger)

**By far** the busiest intermediate station was Kirk Michael, some 7¼ miles from St John's. It had a goods shed, a siding and raised cattle dock, all of which are visible in this view of No. 14 *Thornhill* arriving from Ramsey during the afternoon of 27 May 1959. The various wagons suggest there may still have been some limited freight activity, although the cattle pen looks to be disused. Attached to it is a large poster advertising Glen Wyllin. (Marcus Eavis/Online Transport Archive)

**An excellent** view of summer crowds alighting from a six-coach train on 19 August 1960. Most will have a return ticket, probably including admission to the Glen. The park, which catered for all ages, offered a wide range of attractions, some of which were added after the site was acquired by the IMR in 1935. As there were no platforms at Kirk Michael, the track ballast was at rail level so as to form a reasonably smooth surface. This was a common feature across the network and explained why so many of the carriages were fitted with two footboards. A few minutes later, No. 5 will continue on its way to Ramsey. At this time, *Mona* was a regular on the Peel and Ramsey lines.

(Les Folkard/Online Transport Archive)

**In contrast** to the previous view, all is quiet during the early afternoon of 17 July 1964 except for a couple of passengers waiting patiently for the ex-County Donegal railcars to depart for Douglas at 4pm. On view are the typical, well-constructed MNR Station, its goods shed and a solitary wagon. The path down to Glen Wyllin Park is on the other side of the crossing gates. Although there had been a passing place here since the opening of the line, it was subsequently extended over the level crossing in order to accommodate longer trains.

(Marcus Eavis/Online Transport Archive)

**This was** the sight none of the railway's many supporters wished to see (or photograph), but scenes like these are an integral part of the overall history. After lying fallow for several years, the northern lines were dismantled during the mid-1970s. On 25 August 1975, contractors are loading scrap metal onto a lorry at Kirk Michael. Fortunately, the Station building and goods shed survived – still used today by the local fire service – as well as a few other relics.

(G. W. Price)

**Most people** are busily looking back to check the crossing gates have been closed as No. 10 *G.H.Wood* prepares to leave Ballaugh with the 10.47 St John's–Ramsey on 3 June 1968. This once busy station was located 10 miles from St John's. By the end, one of the tracks of the former passing loop, which had extended over the level crossing, was clearly out of use. After closure, the Station building was demolished, but the goods shed and part of the cattle dock (right) still survive. (Bernard Harrison, courtesy Bob Bridger)

**In an** attempt to attract more custom, a new stop was introduced during the 1965 season. Named Ballavolley Halt, it provided access to Curragh's Wildlife Park, a new government-sponsored attraction. However, there was no platform and no facilities, so intending passengers had to clamber down onto the trackside, as seen in this view of No. 12 *Hutchinson* taken in August 1968. (Hamish Stevenson)

**Like many** MNR stations, Sulby Bridge, 13 miles from St John's, had a substantial Station building with booking office and waiting rooms, although, by the end, its former passing loop and siding had been lifted. Overlooked by a palm tree, No. 10 is on the final leg of its journey with the 10.47am from St John's to Ramsey on 3 June 1968, the crew having kindly allowed the photographer to alight at various locations to take pictures. During much of the 1960s, and especially during the final two seasons, all too often the only passengers were enthusiasts, some of whom had come from overseas to ride the little trains. The majority of local residents had long deserted the infrequent rail service, preferring instead the bus or their own private cars. Even the subsidised school journeys on the Ramsey line had been terminated in the early 1960s. (Bernard Harrison, courtesy Bob Bridger)

**In the** photographer's notes, this view of No. 4 *Loch* is said to be at 'Sulby Bridge' and forms one of a group of three taken at the same location on 3 August 1964. It is clearly not the Station itself, although people appear to be clambering down onto the trackside. In all probability some passengers may have failed to get off at the Station and the train has pulled up to allow them to alight, or it could be that the locomotive has failed (an all-too-frequent occurrence at this time) and some passengers have decided to make alternative arrangements. However, it did allow the photographer to also jump down and record the scene. (Charles Firminger, courtesy Bob Bridger)

**Ramsey had** been the administrative headquarters of the MNR, and No. 14 *Thornhill* (former MNR No. 3) is seen arriving at the Terminal Station with a short mixed train on 27 May 1959. Journey time from Douglas was 1 hour and 20 minutes, and from St John's 47 minutes. As at Douglas, the railway occupied a considerable amount of land. (Marcus Eavis/Online Transport Archive)

**Although the** branch to the harbour had been abandoned some years ago, and the movement of cattle to and from the weekly market had also ended, the large yard still handled some freight in May 1959. After uncoupling from its train, No. 14 is shown shunting three M-series wagons, the last of which, M32, is loaded with some particularly noxious-looking oil drums. On-site facilities included a goods shed, carriage shed, locomotive shed, ore shed, cattle dock, coal stack and water tower. (Marcus Eavis/Online Transport Archive)

**In the** summer of 1968, No. 10 *G.H.Wood* stands at the entrance to the stone-built locomotive shed and workshop. The water tower was located on the left and the line to the station on the right. After each trip, the locomotive would take on coal and water before returning south. Running repairs were also undertaken here. At different times over the years, locomotives such as Nos 1, 8 and 14 were out-shedded here.

(Alan Murray-Rust/Online Transport Archive)

**In July** 1956, No. 10 *G.H.Wood* and No. 8 *Fenella* have good heads of steam as they prepare to leave for Douglas. The front carriage is one of the 'Pairs'. Again, this has probably been added to provide additional seating capacity. Alongside is the primitive-looking, corrugated-iron carriage shed. On the platform are some mailbags. The lighting is provided by two different types of lamp, including some with unusual concrete bases. (John McCann/Online Transport Archive)

**This view** shows the wide island platform with its bay on the south side, occupied on this occasion by No. 10, which is shunting a short train consisting of a G-series van and one of the 'Empress Vans'. A policeman, in his distinctive white helmet, is keeping a watchful eye on the proceedings.

(Alan Murray-Rust/Online Transport Archive)

**This view** shows part of Ramsey Station which also housed the administrative offices of the MNR. The single-storey, brick-built building had a wooden canopy extending over part of the main platform. In August 1964, No. 8 *Fenella* is preparing to leave bunker-first with the 1.45pm departure for Douglas. In the late 1970s, the whole derelict site was eventually cleared to make way for a new industrial complex, principally the Ramsey Bakery.

(Marcus Eavis/Online Transport Archive)

**Situated within** walking distance of Ramsey Station (and the Manx Electric Railway terminus) was the half-mile-long Queen's Pier. Opened in 1886, it added considerably to the town's potential as a tourist centre as passenger steamers to or from Belfast and Ardrossan were now able to directly serve the burgeoning resort. During its construction, a 3ft-gauge tramway was laid along the pier itself for the movement of building materials. On completion, the tramway was used to convey luggage from the steamer to the street and vice versa. Then, when a new landing stage was opened in 1899, a small passenger car was introduced onto the tramway. All these early four-wheel vehicles were hand-propelled until 1937 when the IOM Harbour Board purchased an 8hp petrol-driven Hibberd 'Planet' locomotive and bogie trailer complete with protective wooden shutters. This combination is seen approaching the sea end of the pier on 6 June 1965. (E. J. McWatt/Online Transport Archive)

**To handle** post-war demand, the Harbour Board acquired a Wickham railcar, powered by a Ford petrol engine, in 1950. Painted in a predominantly green livery, the 11-seater waits to leave the sea end of the pier on 10 June 1957. At this time the single fare for an adult was 2d and for a child 1d. Note one of the four hand-propelled luggage 'flat cars' on the right side of the two-track Terminus. (John McCann/Online Transport Archive)

**The tramway** had one loop, where both units were photographed in May 1961. By now, the railcar was in a cream and red livery. When on the move, this unit created an ear-shattering racket as it vibrated noisily along the rails. (Phil Tatt/Online Transport Archive)

**This view,** taken on 15 September 1963, shows the protective metal shutters on the railcar, which by this time was painted red with white roof and trim. Fares had doubled since 1957. The Wickham tended to be used during the quieter times between the arrival and departure of the steamers, usually carrying visitors and residents, including anglers. (Brian Faragher/Online Transport Archive)

**When steamers** stopped calling at Ramsey at the end of the 1970 season, the tramway continued to operate, sometimes spasmodically, until the end of the 1981 season after which the Wickham unit was broken up. This view, taken in September 1975, shows virtually the full length of the line looking from the landward end. After closure, the recently-rebuilt and re-engined Hibberd locomotive and trailer were eventually passed to the IOM Railway Society, and this preserved combination still sees occasional use on short sections of the MER. (Derek Norman/Online Transport Archive)

**Colour views** of the Groudle Glen Railway in the early 1950s are uncommon. Since its opening in 1896, the mile-long, 2ft-gauge line has enjoyed something of a chequered history. Built to transport visitors from the Glen to the ocean, the line terminated at Sea Lion Rocks. Over the years, attractions included a zoo, an enclosure for polar bears (until the First World War) and another for sea lions (until the Second World War), plus a cafe. Power was initially provided by the suitably-named *Sea Lion* and during an enthusiast visit on 2 August 1953, this recently-overhauled locomotive was posed outside the workshop at Llen Coan Station.
(Jim Jarvis/Kidderminster Railway Museum)

**The motive** power provided for the enthusiasts' special on 2 August 1953 was *Polar Bear*, which dated from 1905. Like *Sea Lion*, this 2-4-0 tank engine was built by W. G. Bagnall & Co. of Stafford. Here it is standing at The Headland with half the fleet of eight four-wheel carriages built by G. F. Milnes of Birkenhead between 1896 and 1905. Owing to a rock fall, trains only ran as far as this point when the line finally reopened in 1950, after being closed on the outbreak of war. (Jim Jarvis/Kidderminster Railway Museum)

**With its** highly-polished boiler bands, colourful red and blue livery, and its name picked out in yellow, *Polar Bear* is seen again at The Headland shortly before the line closed at the end of the 1958 season. Trains did not run again until ownership of the Glen changed hands in 1960, after which *Polar Bear* provided an advertised summer service during the 1961/2 seasons. When the locomotive failed, no service was provided in 1963 and subsequently the railway fell into a state of disrepair. Despite the track being lifted, and locomotives and rolling stock being dispersed or vandalised, a dedicated band of volunteers ensured that this charming line with its magnificent vistas was eventually reopened in 1986. *Polar Bear* itself spent time at the Brockham Museum in Surrey and, later, at the Amberley Museum and Heritage Centre in West Sussex where it saw occasional use, and where it remains today. However, this little locomotive has paid short return visits to the Groudle Glen Railway on three occasions, most recently in 2005. (Phil Tatt/Online Transport Archive)

**For a** period, *Sea Lion* could be seen in a somewhat parlous state at the Isle of Man Steam Centre at Kirk Michael where this view was taken in July 1971. With support from British Nuclear Fuels, the locomotive was restored in 1986/7 and has operated on the Groudle line since then.

(M. C. Cunningham/Online Transport Archive)

**Realising that** newly-emerging, competing bus companies were threatening to drain traffic from the railways, the IMR started its own bus services in 1928 using the fleet name Isle of Man Road Services, with both bus and rail operations being administered by the same Manager, A. M. Sheard. It quickly bought out its main competitors and a subsidiary limited company was formed in 1930. Two examples of the early bus fleet survive to this day, the oldest being MN5105, a Leyland Lion PLSC1 with 28-seat Massey body dating from 1927. This had been ordered by Cumberland Motor Services, but diverted to its Manxland Bus Services subsidiary, which sold out to the Railway in 1929. Eventually numbered 49 in the Road Services fleet, it was retained as a tree lopper after withdrawal in 1951 and given the number 117. After being put in store in 1967, it was transferred to Isle of Man National Transport Ltd (IOMNT) in 1976. It now forms part of the Isle of Man Transport (IOMT)/ Bus Vannin heritage fleet and is an unrestored exhibit at Jurby Transport Museum. This view was taken in Douglas Garage in 1963.

(Alan Murray-Rust/Online Transport Archive)

**The second** survivor is MN5454, a Thornycroft A2 with Hall Lewis 28-seat body, acquired by the IMR in 1928 as No. 13. When withdrawn in 1949, it became a towing vehicle and was renumbered 116. It too passed to IOMNT and was seen here some years earlier in Douglas Garage. Now part of the IOMT heritage fleet, this veteran remains operable and still makes occasional appearances. (Alan Murray-Rust/Online Transport Archive)

**There now** follows a selection of images covering the different types of Road Services vehicles operated until 1976 when IOMNT came into being. The first two views represent the batch of six Leyland Lion LT9 single-deckers delivered in 1938 with Leyland rear-entrance bodies. When delivered they adhered to the seating limitation of 28 for any bus operating outside Douglas, but when this was altered the following year to 34, they were fitted with an additional 6 seats. In the first scene, No. 37 is parked across the road from the bus depot in Ramsey, whilst in the second No. 47 was in the yard at Port Erin Garage on 25 May 1959. Note the pen on the roof for carrying luggage. They are in the Road Services livery of red and cream with black lining – officially Tekaloid 'bright red' and 'broken white'. When withdrawn in 1964, both vehicles ended their lives in static use in farmers' fields where they survived for many years. (John L. May/Online Transport Archive: Marcus Eavis/Online Transport Archive)

**Despite a** large increase in the Island's wartime population, the first new buses to arrive were six utility Bedford OWBs with standard 32-seat, forward-entrance Duple bodies which were delivered in July 1945. These formed the only major group of non-Leyland vehicles acquired new by IOMRS. In this June 1962 photograph, No. 26 is shown at Port Erin. Withdrawn some four years later, it was used for some time by a motor cycle club at Castletown. (F. W. Ivey)

**In this** view, No. 27 is entering Lord Street Bus Station in Douglas. When withdrawn in the mid-1960s, it was operated by IMR until February 1968 as Parcel Van 118, after which it ended its days as a hen house.

(John L. May/Online Transport Archive)

**Here, No.** 39 rests between duties at Lord Street Bus Station. All six of these Bedford OWBs (26–29 and 39–40) remained virtually unaltered until withdrawn during 1966/7, with No. 39 ending its days as another hen house.

(John L. May/Online Transport Archive)

**At the** core of Manager Sheard's post-war renewal programme was the purchase of significant numbers of double-deckers, of which the first example, an all-Leyland PD1 with a 56-seat body, arrived in 1946. However, at the time, Manx law prohibited the operation of vehicles with more than 34 seats outside Douglas so, until the law was rapidly repealed, No. 3 worked on the Onchan circular service with all but eight of its upper-deck seats roped off. Eleven PD1As entered service during 1947 with bodies built to standard Leyland specifications by Lancashire Aircraft (4, 6–8, 10–12) and Salmesbury (15, 16, 23, 24). Although No. 12 was withdrawn in 1958 due to accident damage, the last of this class lingered on until 1972. On 23 May 1959 No. 4 is passing through St John's en route to Peel with Tynwald Church in the background. This trunk route from Douglas ran in direct competition with the less-frequent rail service. (Marcus Eavis/Online Transport Archive)

**Here, No.** 16, one of the four Leyland PD1As with Salmesbury bodies, stands outside Ramsey Garage. A lady with a poodle consults the timetable. (R. L. Wilson/Online Transport Archive)

**Sheard's regeneration** programme also involved the acquisition of new single-deckers which were needed for less-well-patronised routes or for those restricted to single-deck operation only, owing to low bridges such as the one at Lower Foxdale on the St John's to Castletown road. First to arrive were four Leyland Tiger PS1/1s with 35-seat, rear-entrance Eastern Coachworks bodies which entered service in 1948, although the chassis had been manufactured in 1946. In this view No. 57 is preparing to turn out of Atholl Street in Peel. It was withdrawn in 1967 together with Nos 34, 52 and 58, the other three Tigers. No. 34 is privately preserved on the Island.

(John L. May/Online Transport Archive)

**Between 1949** and 1951 a further twenty-two double-deckers entered service. These were all-Leyland PD2s with 56-seat bodies. The first three were taken out of service in 1968, the same year in which some of the survivors were renumbered, whilst the bulk were withdrawn between 1970 and 1976. Seen in the original version of the double-deck livery, No. 1 is at Jurby Airport on 1 July 1966. The bus displays an attractive advert for Cambrian Air Services detailing some of the destinations on offer. When a more logical fleet numbering scheme replaced the random 'fill-in-the-gaps' policy in 1968, No. 1 became No. 73. Three of these vehicles survived long enough to pass to IOMNT in 1976, although this one went straight for scrap when withdrawn in 1972. No. 2 (later No. 74) is retained in the IOMT heritage fleet. Two others survive in the UK, but both in non-authentic liveries to replicate long-scrapped vehicles. (Brian Faragher/Online Transport Archive)

**The first** underfloor-engined buses to appear on the Island were eight rare Leyland Olympic HR40s of integral chassis-less construction fitted with 40-seat Weymann bodies and which entered service during 1950/1. Some were renumbered in 1968, and all were withdrawn between 1972 and 1975. In this scene, No. 18 (later 47) was photographed at St John's on 12 September 1968. This was the last of the Olympics to be withdrawn and was eventually scrapped in 1979 after being sold to a dealer. One of the group, No. 84, has been preserved on the Island.
(Brian Faragher/Online Transport Archive)

**In the** same year Sheard took delivery of the Olympics, he purchased another Bedford OB with Mulliner bodywork, an earlier example, No. 25, having been acquired in 1948. Seen in Lord Street Bus Station, Douglas, on 6 September 1963, No. 43 was withdrawn in 1967. It became a Parcel Van until 1969 after which it ended its days as yet another hen house. In contrast to the early utility OWB, the superior Mulliner body had chrome window surrounds and full-width driver's windscreen. Also, the cream band had an attractive little upward flick at the front end.

(Brian Faragher/Online Transport Archive)

**As part** of the takeover of J. Broadbent's Safeway Service from Ramsey to Kirk Michael in 1950, three single-deckers were added to the Road Services fleet, two of which are seen in colour. The oldest of the trio was given the number 86. Dating from 1944, it was a Bedford OWB with Duple 30-seat body and is seen here at the rear of Ramsey Depot in 1963.

(John L. May/Online Transport Archive)

**In May** 1961, the same vehicle was photographed coming out of Port Erin Garage. The conductor is already sporting his summer dust coat. After withdrawal in 1966, the vehicle served briefly as a railway parcels van before being sold as another hen house.

(Phil Tatt/Online Transport Archive)

**Also acquired** from Broadbent's was an unusual Commer Commando with a 32-seat Waveney body, which was given the fleet number 87.
This had been new to Hirst Tours of Longwell in 1947, the year before it was acquired by Broadbent's. With Tynwald Hill as the backdrop, No.
87 is waiting to leave St John's for Peel. (John L. May/Online Transport Archive)

**After being** withdrawn in 1966, No. 87 became railway Parcels Van No. 120 and, in this rare view taken on 6 July 1966, it is shown with its new fleet number, turning towards the Station yard at Douglas. After serving in this capacity for a very short time it was sold off in 1967, becoming another hen house. The Bedford M-series lorry on the right was owned by a local window cleaner. (Brian Faragher/Online Transport Archive)

**Four all-Leyland** Royal Tigers with 44-seat forward-entrance bodies entered service in 1952. These were the first eight-foot wide IOMRS buses and whilst they had the same engine and running gear as the earlier Olympics, they had a separate chassis. To offer an improved service to and from Ronaldsway Airport, the seating on Nos 88–91 was later reduced to 40 and luggage racks were fitted. However, in 1974 these Royal Tigers were again fitted with 44 seats and No. 90 is seen outside Peel Garage, by which time it had been equipped for one-man operation. After passing to IOMNT, all four were withdrawn during 1977/8. At least one of the four survives in preservation. (W. Ryan)

**No further** new buses were delivered until 1956 when three Leyland Titan PD2s (Nos 93–95) with 62-seat somewhat spartan Metro-Cammell Orion-style bodies entered service, one of which (No. 93) is seen here on private hire at Ronaldsway Airport on 18 July 1964. After withdrawal some ten years later, No. 93 was sold to a dealer at Jurby and scrapped by 1977. This batch, fitted with Midland Red (BMMO) 'tin-fronts', were the first double-deckers to have the simplified livery with just a single cream band. (Marcus Eavis/Online Transport Archive)

**Three further** double-deckers (31–33) followed in 1958. These were Leyland Titan PD3s with 73-seat Metro-Cammell Orion-style bodies making them the largest vehicles on the Island. They were fitted with the 'tin-front' grilles originally specified by Midland Red, and the space on the grille for the initials BMMO is clearly visible on this view of No. 33 tackling the hill between Laxey and South Cape on 24 May 1959. After passing to IOMNT, these PD3s were withdrawn in 1982. No. 32 is preserved in IOMT's heritage fleet and No. 31 is also believed to survive, as an open-topper in Spain.

(Marcus Eavis/Online Transport Archive)

**Two batches** of Leyland Tiger Cubs were acquired – the first four, Nos 19–22, arriving in 1957 with 44-seat Weymann bodies. No. 20 is seen here shortly after delivery, waiting outside the Regal and Santa Rosa hotels on Douglas Promenade. Between 1961 and 1963, three of the group (Nos 20–22) were converted into dual-purpose 40-seaters for excursion and private-hire work, whilst No. 19 was provided with luggage racks and reduced seating for airport duties. Between 1969 and 1971, Nos 20–22 were painted in a special grey and red coach livery before reverting to normal bus livery the following year. No. 20 is now preserved on the Island.

(John L. May/Online Transport Archive)

**Three more** Tiger Cubs, Nos 54–56, were delivered in 1961 with dual-purpose 41-seat Willowbrook bodies, as seen in this view of No. 56 at Port Erin. (Phil Tatt/Online Transport Archive)

**This view** of No. 55 illustrates the grey and red livery eventually applied to all seven Tiger Cubs. Note the antimacassars over each headrest. Although IOMRS had not previously invested specifically in coaches, many of the fleet were used to transport thousands of summer visitors to hotels and holiday camps, especially on Saturdays. (R. L. Wilson/Online Transport Archive)

**The seven** Tiger Cubs delivered between 1957 and 1961 were later reseated as buses and converted for one-man operation. This view of No. 20 was taken at Laxey shortly before Nos 19–22 were renumbered 5–8 in 1974. They were withdrawn in 1976, but, together with Nos. 54–56, they all passed to the new nationalised bus company, after which Nos 5–8 were restored to passenger service. All were withdrawn again between 1979 and 1981. No. 54 is now at the Jurby Transport Museum in the north of the Island where it awaits restoration. (Peter Deegan)

**This was** one of the three Leyland PD3As (59–61) with 73-seat Metro-Cammell Orion-style bodies and the 'St Helens' front. This view has been included because it shows brand-new No. 59 waiting to be winched from Liverpool Landing Stage onto the IOMSPCo vessel *Peveril* in July 1964. Of special interest are the attachments on the wheels for use by the winch. En route from the manufacturer, it carried neither a fleet name nor a number. By 1970, these buses were reregistered and renumbered 67–69, and as such passed to IOMNT, eventually being withdrawn during 1983/4. No. 67 (the former No. 60) is preserved by Isle of Man Transport. (J. N. Barlow/Online Transport Archive)

**In 1965,** Manager Sheard passed away and was succeeded by W. T. Lambden. He effected savings by pruning unprofitable routes, introducing more one-man operation and some 'Limited-Stop' services. He also developed the coaching side. This was predominantly contract work with IOMRS providing vehicles required by British tour operators to ferry tourists round the Island. To this end, three Leyland Leopards (96–98) with 41-seat dual-purpose Willowbrook bodies entered service in 1967. No. 96 is shown on 30 August of that year at Ramsey in the distinctive coach livery. Although successful, the coaching side passed to Tours (IOM) Ltd in early 1972 along with the three Leopards. A year later, they returned to the Road Services fleet, and were painted in standard red and cream for use on stage services. After becoming part of the IOMNT fleet in 1976, this trio survived for another ten years, and No. 97 itself was bought for preservation on withdrawal.

(Brian Faragher/Online Transport Archive)

**Faced by** mounting costs, increased car ownership and dwindling visitor numbers, Lambden opted to exploit the second-hand market in order to replace the antiquated post-war Bedford OWBs. In 1967, he acquired seven Aldershot & District Dennis Falcons built in 1956 with Gardner engines and forward-entrance 30-seat Strachan bodies. All but two entered service in their Aldershot livery with the addition of a red fleet name panel and new fleet and registration numbers. In this scene, No. 23 is shown at St John's shortly after delivery on 11 September 1968.

(Brian Faragher/Online Transport Archive)

**By 1969,** Nos 23–29 were all in Road Services livery and this view shows No. 28 at St John's on the service to Cronk-y-Voddy in July 1973. Note the position of the fleet number. All the Falcons were withdrawn between 1972 and 1974, with 23 and 28 being amongst the last to go. The latter was sold, but No. 23 was transferred, together with two others, to IOMNT in withdrawn condition in 1976. No. 29 eventually returned to the UK for restoration to its original guise as Aldershot & District No. 282 (POR428). (Peter Deegan)

**To provide** additional capacity, Lambden acquired some full-specification Leyland Leopard and Bristol RE coaches. Four were Bristol RELH6Ls delivered during 1970/1, Nos 37/38 having bodies by Duple Northern and Nos 39/40 by Plaxton. This rare view shows Duple-bodied No. 37 leaving Douglas Bus Station with a lightly-loaded excursion in April 1971. When IOMRS ceased coaching operations, Nos 37 and 38 were based at Ramsey Garage for ordinary service work during 1972, but all four were sold the following year to National Bus Company subsidiary Samuelson's of London. Its successor, National Travel (South East), operated them until 1976, after which they separately spent the rest of their service lives with a variety of independent operators. With its UK registration SGF483L, the former No. 40 is currently stored by an Essex coach operator with a view to a future restoration. (Peter Deegan)

**To replace** more life-expired double-deckers, Lambden looked for further second-hand vehicles, preferring front-engined buses. He believed these to be less expensive to maintain and operate than the new rear-engined designs, and bargains were available. For example, after taking over Stratford Blue, Midland Red had buses for disposal and, as a result, fifteen 73-seat Leyland PD3s were acquired in 1971/2, all of which were built between 1960 and 1966. These were the Island's first second-hand double-deckers and the first in the Road Services fleet with forward entrances. They carried the simplified Lambden livery with the less ornate *'Road Services'* fleet name. No. 71 of 1966, one of eleven with Willowbrook bodies, is shown here at the new ferry terminal in Douglas in 1974. (Phil Tatt/Online Transport Archive)

**The other** four of the ex-Stratford Blue PD3s had exposed radiators (rather than St Helens fronts) and bodies built by Northern Counties. In this view, No. 57 has stopped to pick up passengers on Douglas Promenade. All the ex-Stratford Blue vehicles passed to IOMNT in 1976. In 1979, No. 57 was one of three of the Northern Counties buses (57–59) to be converted into open-toppers, the last being withdrawn at the end of the 1983 season. Two of the open-toppers are believed to survive – one in Ireland and one in the Netherlands. (W. Ryan)

**1974 was** marked by the arrival of a further ten second-hand double-deckers, this time from Bournemouth Corporation Transport. Again these were Leyland PD3s, but this time with 69-seat Weymann bodies dating from 1963. Reregistered and allocated the fleet numbers 72–81, they passed to IOMNT in 1976 where they were again renumbered and lasted until 1983/4. No. 76 is shown shortly after entering service in Castletown, by which time much of the Bournemouth front destination display was not in use. Many returned to the UK after service on the Island. Two survive, one of which has been superbly restored to Bournemouth colours. (W. Ryan)

**After a** gap of several years, orders were placed for new buses, but only after the Government offered financial support. Fourteen 52-seat Leyland Nationals were delivered between 1974 and 1976. The first to arrive was No. 14, and a month after entering service in April 1974 this bus was reregistered from MN9514 to MAN14A, as is shown here when on its way to Port Jack.
(Phil Tatt/Online Transport Archive)

**Shown here** is the brand-new No. 16 at Lord Street Bus Station in Douglas on 28 June 1975. All the Nationals passed to IOMNT in 1976. Despite problems with the engine and the saloon heating, they provided reliable service during the 1980s and, with the exception of one accident victim, all survived well into the 1990s. (R. L. Wilson/Online Transport Archive)

**The 15¾-mile** line from Douglas to Port Erin must now be one of the most photographed narrow-gauge lines in the world. However, for much of the 1960s and 1970s, its future was very much in the balance. In a desperate attempt to improve ridership, it was rebranded under the Lord Ailsa regime as *'The Isle of Man Victorian Steam Railway'*. However, when the Marquess took the option to cancel his lease after five years, the IMR found itself again in charge with limited financial backing from the Tourist Board. As described earlier, the northern lines never reopened after the 1968 season and, for a period, it seemed as if the southern line would suffer the same fate, especially when trains operated only over the outer end for the 1975 and 1976 seasons. Fortunately, after the IMR was nationalised in 1977, the railway was placed on a more stable financial footing. In this view taken during the Ailsa period, one of the locomotives has just left Douglas and is working hard as it tackles the steep grade up Nunnery Bank on 28 August 1968. (John McCann/Online Transport Archive)

**Having cleared** the wooded area, the long climb continues up to the summit at Keristal where passengers can look towards the sea and the Marine Drive. On 3 August 1953, No. 14 *Thornhill* is assisted by No. 16 *Mannin* as it storms up the two-mile climb towards Port Soderick with the first train of the day, the 10.10am from Douglas to Port Erin. Amongst the carriages are three 'Pairs' including F63. Note the different liveries with the cream extending well below the windows on some. Usually the banking engine simply dropped off once the summit had been cleared, but where it had been coupled up it then had to be uncoupled by the fireman edging along the locomotive whilst on the move. (John McCann/Online Transport Archive)

**Taken nearly** twenty-five years later on 4 July 1977, No. 13 *Kissack* tackles the grade on Port Soderick Bank, but with a much shorter five-coach train. This was the first year in which trains once more ran the full length of the line. (Andrew King)

Located 3½ miles from Douglas, Port Soderick is now a pale shadow of the once-popular beach resort which, in its heyday, was served by the railway, the Douglas Head Marine Drive Electric Tramway and small steam ships. In times past, demand was so heavy that double-headed trains often ran to and from Douglas, and the long curving platform (right) was built for departing passengers on the north side. On 6 July 1977, the driver of No. 13 *Kissack* looks back, waiting for the all-clear before proceeding towards Douglas.
(Andrew King)

Reflecting the importance of Port Soderick, the IMR replaced the original Station building in 1896 with this elegant structure, which included refreshment facilities as well as accommodation for the station master and his family. On 28 June 1976, No. 4 *Loch* has stopped outside the elegant ivy-clad building with a small works train consisting of a single M-series wagon. The weed-strewn tracks and platform indicate that this rare photograph was taken during the period when the line north of Ballasalla was only used intermittently to provide access to the workshops at Douglas. This Station building was sold in 1984 and the Station subsequently modernised.
(Andrew King)

**The scorched** grass on the slopes of Santon Cutting was the result of fires started by sparks from the locomotives. Here, No. 16 *Mannin* is heading towards Santon Station in July 1956. The body of F44, the leading coach, was scrapped in 1983 and its frames in 2010.

(John McCann/Online Transport Archive)

**Santon is** one of the stations modernised in recent years with improved track layouts and half-height platforms. Always a favourite with photographers, it is still a crossing point, the loop having existed since the mid-1870s together with the small wooden building on the down side. From its opening there was a siding also serving a cattle dock. Unfortunately, in more recent years, local residents rarely board at Santon. On 3 July 1978, No. 11 *Maitland* departs for Port Erin. Only the up track is in use, the other being occupied by the County Donegal railcars, now relegated to works duties, as well as a wagon filled with ballast. (Andrew King)

**The Port** Erin line has a number of road, path and farm-track crossings, often in isolated locations. During the period covered by this book, the majority of these were manned, and small huts or cottages were provided for the gatekeepers whose job it was to open and close the gates. Usually, the locomotive would sound its whistle when some distance away, allowing ample time for the gates to be opened and the crossing keeper to give visual confirmation that the train could proceed. During the winter, the locomotive crews would often drop off lumps of coal for the gate keepers. Here, a train passes slowly through Ballalonna Crossing on the south side of Santon in July 1973. The small wooden hut with its corrugated iron roof is now disused. (Peter Deegan)

**A main** crossing point still exists at Ballasalla, which is some 8½ miles from Douglas and is the first village of any size on the journey south. This view of No. 11 *Maitland* was taken on 28 June 1976. This was the season when trains were limited to running between Ballasalla and Port Erin. In readiness for the return journey, the crew are carrying out a routine inspection which involves oiling some of the locomotive's vital components. At the other end of the five-coach train is No. 4 *Loch*. Fortunately, the through service to Douglas was restored in time for the 1977 season. The long-term future of the railway was finally secured when the line was nationalised prior to the 1978 season, and work also began on relaying track and modernising stations. By the end of the 1970s, all of the Island's main transport, except for the horse trams operated by Douglas Corporation, had fallen under the jurisdiction of Isle of Man Passenger Transport. (Andrew King)

**When through** services were restored along the south line for the 1977 season, Ballasalla again became a passing point. On 23 September 1977, the station master waits to hand the token for the single-track section to the driver of a train from Port Erin. Note the oil cans on the buffer beam of No. 13 *Kissack* and the 1893-built Gibbins breakdown crane in the background. This was subsequently fully restored and can now be seen at the former Union Mills Station. This view shows the typical IMR wooden station building with its corrugated iron roof. There was also a cattle dock and the wooden goods shed which had once been part of the First World War internment camp at Knockaloe. This area was cleared for redevelopment in the 1980s and was replaced by a new station complete with platforms. (Andrew King)

**On leaving** Ballasalla, southbound trains have to cross the main road to Ronaldsway Airport, located at the west end of the Station. The volume of road traffic makes this by far the busiest level crossing on the line. On 7 July 1977, No. 11 *Maitland* whistles as it passes the crossing keeper's cottage and the manually-operated gates. Today, the crossing has automatic barriers. (Andrew King)

**Located just** under 10 miles from Douglas, Castletown Station is some 10 minutes walk from the ancient capital, one-time home of the Kings of Mann. As many visitors still use the railway to reach the town, it is by far the busiest intermediate station and still retains its passing loop. On 25 May 1959, Marcus Eavis took this view of No. 8 *Fenella* arriving from Douglas and passing a small amount of goods waiting to be loaded by the Station staff. The elegant stone goods shed (right) which had replaced the original wooden building in 1902, had access from both ends as well as doors at both rail and platform level. When all goods traffic ceased in 1969, it was retained for storage and other purposes, and still stands today. (Marcus Eavis/Online Transport Archive)

**During his** visit on 25 May 1959, Marcus Eavis recorded this view of No. 5 *Mona* approaching Castletown, smokebox-first, with a train from Port Erin. During most of the year, three or four carriages were the norm, but some trains could have nine or more, and if No. 16 *Mannin* was not available, these were often banked or double-headed. Amongst those carrying the heaviest loads were the Douglas *'Boat Trains'* which connected with certain seasonal sailings. (Marcus Eavis/Online Transport Archive)

**There were** signals on sections of this line, but movements over the single-track sections relied upon the use of tokens. In 1967, a young enthusiast was observing the station master handing the token to the driver of a Douglas-bound train, giving him permission to proceed into the next section.
(E. C. Bennett/Online Transport Archive)

**Although there** was talk of reopening the Peel line to mark the 100th anniversary of the Island's first railway, this was deemed impractical as it would have meant transferring vital resources away from the more economically-viable Port Erin line. In the event, the Peel centenary was marked by a static display of locomotives at Douglas Station and by the operation of a special commemorative train which ran from Port Erin to Douglas on Sunday, 1 July 1973. Earlier that day, this train passed through Castletown Station under the watchful eye of the station master and some excited local residents. The board advertising the anniversary was displayed on the rear of *Kissack,* but it would not be unveiled until the special was ready to leave Port Erin later in the day. At the front of the long, eleven-coach train is No. 10 *G.H.Wood.* When this stone-built Station with its twin gables was upgraded in the early 1990s, the wooden canopy (left) was removed and half-height platforms installed.
(Brian Faragher/Online Transport Archive)

**Just west** of Castletown Station is a stone overbridge spanning the Silverburn River, a favourite location for photographers. This view of No. 16 *Mannin* was taken in August 1963, by which time this powerful locomotive was looking ever more shabby, and was in urgent need of a major overhaul and boiler replacement.
(Derek Norman/Online Transport Archive)

**In May** 1961, No. 11 *Maitland* was approaching Castletown bunker-first with a train from Port Erin.
(Phil Tatt/Online Transport Archive)

**In this** shot, taken on 27 June 1976, No. 4 *Loch* powers towards Port St Mary, having just passed over the Mill Road level crossing. The gates, which are visible in the background, were manned until 2001 when automatic barriers operated from Castletown Station were installed. The 1970s were a worrying time for the southern line. Following the end of the Ailsa lease, the railway was subsidised by the Tourist Board for the 1972–74 seasons, after which financial responsibility reverted to the IMR. In order to save money, they curtailed the service to run between Port Erin and Castletown during the 1975 season, and then, following some vigorous campaigning, as far as Ballasalla for the following season. When this view was taken, the future looked very uncertain. (Andrew King)

**Some 12¾** miles from Douglas is the Station serving the small town of Colby, where this view was taken in June 1965. The train was entering the platform-less passing loop, having just crossed the little-used level crossing. Another crossing also existed at the other end of this Station. Today, Colby has been spruced up and is now home to the former passenger shelter relocated from Braddan. (Photographer unknown/LRTA (London Area)/Online Transport Archive)

**The centenary** of the Port Erin line was marked twice – first on 1 August 1974, and then a week later when the Lieutenant Governor was able to attend. On the second occasion, *Loch* was suitably decorated as it passed Ballagawne Crossing. Amazingly, this same veteran 2-4-0 tank engine had played a part 100 years earlier on the opening day. The gates at this crossing were replaced by automatic barriers in 2002. The former gatekeeper's cottage had been larger than most on the network and included staff accommodation. Note the display of wild meadow flowers. (Andrew King)

**Just under** 15 miles from Douglas is the Station serving the small resort and harbour at Port St Mary. Trains arriving from the Colby direction first crossed the road leading down to the village. In this evocative 1974 scene, the approaching train can be seen whistling in the far distance, with the home signal down and the gatekeeper in the process of opening the gates. His shelter (right) is now in private hands and the gates have been replaced by barriers, complete with audible warnings and lights to control the road traffic. (Phil Tatt/Online Transport Archive)

**A richly-atmospheric** view of No. 16 *Mannin* pausing at Port St Mary in early August 1953 with a well-loaded train for Port Erin. Although visitor numbers had soared at the end of the Second World War, people began deserting the Island in ever-increasing numbers from the mid-1950s onwards, leading to a sharp decline in revenue for the railway, and the eventual closure of the Peel and Ramsey lines. (Jim Jarvis/Kidderminster Railway Museum)

**As the** tourist trade at Port St Mary developed, the original wooden station was replaced in 1898 by the present two-storey building. After Douglas, this was the largest on the network and boasted a spacious booking office, waiting rooms and upper-level accommodation for the station master. As it is only about a mile from the end of the line no passing loop was provided; however, unlike most of the other stations, it did have a platform. The canopy visible on the right would later be bricked in. On this occasion, the railcars were carrying a party of railway enthusiasts to Port Erin. (Ken Farrell/Online Transport Archive.)

**This view** of the 4pm departure from Douglas was taken from the western end of Port St Mary Station on 25 May 1959. Interestingly, the guard has not yet shut his door as No. 5 *Mona* sets off on the four-minute run to Port Erin. In the background an M-series wagon juts out from the entrance to the large goods shed which was of similar design to the one at Castletown. Just visible on the platform is an IMR lorry. In the 1970s this yard was used for storage purposes when the train service was curtailed at Castletown and later Ballasalla. In 1979, the siding through the shed was lifted, but later reinstated. The impressive red-brick station which still stands today was last used by the IMR in the 1970s, after which the station master was provided with a small wooden hut located on the platform. In recent years, Port St Mary Station has been destaffed. (Marcus Eavis/Online Transport Archive)

**For decades,** the IMR housed and maintained a fleet of lorries at their premises in Douglas. These were used to ferry parcels and other goods between stations and customers. After the Second World War, this once-vital service suffered a serious decline as people found easier and quicker methods of transportation, so when Marcus Eavis took his couple of views on 25 May 1959, he was recording a way of life which would shortly disappear. This close-up of lorry No. 14 was taken on the platform at Port St Mary just after it had arrived from the nearby village.

(Marcus Eavis/Online Transport Archive)

**Earlier in** the afternoon, the photographer had spotted the veteran petrol-driven lorry doing its rounds in Port St Mary. His notes describe it as 'rather the worse for wear'. Perhaps this was not surprising as its Thornycroft A2 chassis was by then over thirty years old. It had started life as a single-decker bus with Manx Motors in 1927 and had a 28-seat Strachan & Brown body. After passing to IMR in early 1929, it became No. 70 in the IOMRS fleet. Then, after withdrawal in 1937, it was eventually converted into lorry No. 14 in July 1945, in which guise it continued to operate until April 1961. (Marcus Eavis/Online Transport Archive)

**The average** journey time from Port Erin to Douglas was 50 minutes, although a few trains did it in slightly less time, and before the Second World War some non-stop expresses were scheduled to complete the journey in just 40 minutes. Situated 15¾ miles from Douglas by rail, Port Erin is one of the most visited towns on the Island, and is renowned for its clear water and scenic vistas. The coming of the railway undoubtedly contributed to its development and the original terminal facilities soon proved inadequate, so major improvements were made at the beginning of the twentieth century. These included additional sidings, a new locomotive shed, water tower, goods shed and station built in Ruabon brick. This fine building had a booking office and waiting rooms. There was also a porter's room as many visitors would have required assistance with their luggage. On 3 August 1953, No. 14 *Thornhill* is waiting to depart from the main platform. The carriages on the right are in the bay platform, later taken over as a bus storage area when the facilities were rationalised. (John McCann/Online Transport Archive)

**In July** 1964, there seems to be more staff than passengers as the guard prepares to load sacks from a trolley and the driver walks round No. 11 *Maitland,* just after it has been coupled to the 11.50am for Douglas. Until the construction of a new, secure, shed in 1998, carriages were parked in the open overnight and were sometimes subjected to acts of vandalism. The road in the foreground was a right of way which cut across the station throat. (Marcus Eavis/ Online Transport Archive)

**One locomotive** was usually housed overnight at Port Erin, ready to work the first train of the morning, which left several hours before the first train arrived from Douglas. This 1967 vista shows the single-road locomotive shed and No. 5 *Mona* standing alongside the water tower. The track on the immediate right led to the goods shed. For a period in the 1980s and 1990s, the goods shed became the locomotive shed, and the latter was used to house withdrawn locomotives such as *Fenella* and *Douglas*. Today, the former goods shed has become the entrance to the Isle of Man Railway Museum which was opened in a former Isle of Man Road Services bus garage in 1975. (Alan Murray-Rust/Online Transport Archive)

**On 1** July 1973, Port Erin was besieged by enthusiasts, residents and visitors all keen to see the special train marking the 100th anniversary of the opening of the Peel line, the Island's first railway. Commemorative tickets were issued and all 11 coaches were packed. Carrying a suitably-worded inscription on its bunker end, No. 13 *Kissack* was assisted at the rear by No. 10 *G.H. Wood* when the train departed at 3.45pm to much cheering, waving and whistling. (Brian Faragher/Online Transport Archive)

**A year** later, the centenary of the Port Erin line itself was also celebrated in style with special trains on both 1 and 8 August 1974. After the official special carrying the Lord Lieutenant had departed on 8 August, it was followed by a four-coach train hauled by No. 10 *G.H. Wood*.
(Andrew King)

**Like the** other terminal stations, the one at Port Erin originally occupied quite a bit of land. The wide open space allowed people to take a variety of photographs whilst waiting for trains. For example, this view of veteran locomotive No. 4 *Loch* in its new maroon livery applied in May 1978 was taken during the following summer.

(John L. May/Online Transport Archive)

**As already** illustrated, centenaries and anniversaries offered the railway management an ideal opportunity to do something different in order to attract residents and visitors. To mark 100 years of the MNR in 1979, the unique 'Foxdale Coach' F39 was repainted in the original MNR colours and renumbered F15.

(John L. May/Online Transport Archive)

**To further** commemorate 100 years of the MNR, No. 13 *Kissack* was painted in the Isle of Man Railway Company's original deep green livery and was photographed waiting to leave Port Erin at the head of a train of four mixed carriages. With the railway now seen by the Government as a vital tourist asset, the future of the Douglas–Port Erin line was at last secure and would continue to provide a timeless reminder of the age of steam for future generations. (John L. May/Online Transport Archive)

## Bibliography

During their research, the authors consulted a range of magazines, timetables, pamphlets, newspaper cuttings, personal memoirs and record books as well as a number of publications, most notably:

*A Century of Manx Transport in Colour*, Robert Hendry, The Manx Experience, 1998.
*Buses of the Isle of Man 1945 – present day*, Richard Davis, Lily Publications.
*Fleet History of the Isle of Man Department of Transport and Tourism*, PSV Circle, 1991.
*Isle of Man Album*, W. J. Wyse and J. Joyce, Ian Allan Publishing, 1968.
*Isle of Man Steam Railway in Colour*, Peter Johnson, Ian Allan Publishing, 1998.
*Isle of Man Railway* (three volumes), J. I. C. Boyd, Oakwood Press, 1993–96.
*Ninety Years of the Ramsey Steamship Company Ltd*, Edward Gray and Roy Fenton, Ships in Focus Publications, 2003.
*Rails in the Isle of Man*, Robert Hendry, Midland Publishing, 1993.
*Railways and Tramways of the Isle of Man*, Ted Gray, Past and Present Publishing, 2008.
*Steam Packet Memories*, John Shepherd, Ferry Publications, 1992.
*The Isle of Man Steam Packet Company Volume 1*, Richard Danielson, The author, 1987.
*The Manx Peacocks*, David Lloyd-Jones, Atlantic, 1998.
*The Railways and Tramways of the Isle of Man*, Barry Edwards, OPC, 1993.
*West Coast Steamers*, Duckworth and Langmuir, T. Stephenson and Sons, 1966.

The *Classic Manx Buses* website has also helped with some of the bus histories.

*Martin Jenkins*
*Walton-on-Thames*

*Charles Roberts*
*Upton, Wirral*

*July 2016*